Way of Now

Nowflow

for meditation,
peak performance,
and daily life

D0103529

Wonchull Park
Mackenzie Hawkins

Publishing

ISBN: 978-1-949706-02-4
Library of Congress Control Number: 2020916241

www.thrupublishing.com

Contents

Preface

"Nowflow"—I remember Master Wonchull Park saying that word in my first class. I thought I knew what he meant. At that time, I'd been meditating for many years so I assumed Master Park was saying what I'd heard many times before: the importance of living in the "here and now" and being "in the flow." I had a lot to learn.

Gradually I realized that "nowflow" is not just another word. It is a way of understanding. With an understanding of nowflow, we can connect the "here and now" of meditation to the "flow state" of peak performance—and everything in between—because nowflow includes all that is practical in action.

Master Park encourages all his students to understand this for ourselves: a simple, general understanding of optimal action. He is a physicist and also a tai chi master. Whatever the situation, there is a way we can allow ourselves to feel better and do better by seeing that we are "in the now" and "in the flow" of nowflow. This is possible by rationally understanding that now includes the flow of change. Because change and our experience of past-present-future do not separate us from now, daily life can be meditation. Peak performance can be daily life. Along with many of Master Park's students, I began to realize that I was learning general answers to age-old questions.

At Master Park's school, there are students who come for the stress-reduction benefits in their daily life. There are students who are interested in meditation or philosophy. There are students who are Kung Fu teachers, boxers, or other athletes and martial artists. We attend classes and practice mostly together. When we talk about how it helps us, someone might mention that they were able to handle a stressful situation calmly and effectively or someone might speak about how they were able to do a powerful one-inch punch in the martial arts.

Master Park has been teaching in this way for over 20 years, and, for about as long, his students have been asking for a book of his teachings. With Master Park's encouragement, I have worked—day by day, draft by draft—to be the scribe that would bring this to others. With every transcription, discussion, and manuscript revision, Master Park guided my writing towards deeper and more general understanding—towards the essential, conundrum-free explanations that could ultimately be most helpful to others.

Way of Now is one of three books—*Way of Now, Mindfulness-in-Action,* and *Relaxation-in-Action*—that can be read in any order or on their own. In Chapter 16 of this book, *Way of Now*, there is some essential explanation on how we can understand mindfulness and relaxation, or wu-wei, generally so that we can also fully apply them to any action. The forthcoming books of *Mindfulness-in-Action* and *Relaxation-in-Action* will go into these topics more in depth, while this book—*Way of Now*—can serve as a foundation of general understanding for the others.

In my own experience and that of many of Master Park's students, this emphasis on general understanding that applies to everything can take some getting used to. For example, when Master Park teaches on nowflow, he's not encouraging us to be "more now" or enticing us with promises of "more flow." He is simply pointing out the way that change fundamentally happens, always. This helps us to see what is always so—no matter what we may try to do. With this foundational understanding that applies to all situations, we can guide ourselves—safely and effectively—as we practice and benefit from various traditions and modalities.

What is this way that we can simply and practically understand for ourselves? How might this help us to have a better performance, a deeper meditation practice, or a calmer day? As we'll see, we can rationally understand nowflow to be the whole of all that makes a practical difference. With this clarity, we can manage any change better.

I hope that this may continue to help so many. That we might feel a wave of relief—because this is something that we can understand for ourselves without relying on unexplained insights. That we can enjoy what is possible for us in life—because we have this under-lying understanding that can carry into all aspects of our lives.

With this hope for us all, it makes me deeply happy to share with you Master Park's teachings on nowflow, related as best I can, in this book, *Way of Now*.

— Mackenzie Hawkins

Princeton, New Jersey
June 2020

Introduction

Two conundrums, one explanation:
nowflow as practical whole

People through the ages have pointed out the many
benefits of being "in the now." When people feel that
they are living "in the now," they tend to feel more
fully alive yet at peace. Many people take up meditation and mindfulness practices in order to discover
that feeling.

Living more "in the now" helps soothe our anxiety
and worry. It may seem, though, that being "in the
now" is not practical in every situation. This can
present a tradeoff or practical conundrum. On the one
hand, living in the "here and now" can help us feel
less stressed and more peaceful. On the other hand,
don't we also need to deal with the past and the future
as we live our lives?

For example, a common meditation instruction is to let
go of thoughts about the past and the future in order
to pay attention to our present-moment experience.

Given this instruction, does living "in the now" mean that we should try to block out thoughts about the past and the future? For the period of a meditation session, trying to "be now" by not thinking about the past and the future might help us feel more calm and ease. Once we are "off the meditation cushion," though, we would need the past and the future to remember and plan—and do what we need to do.

If being now is a matter of blocking out the past and the future, then we would feel as if we need to balance some tradeoff so that we wouldn't take being now too far. With that sense of tradeoff, we could only apply being now to some degree in some situations.

This is a practical conundrum: Being now is helpful, yet fully being now just doesn't seem practical in all activities and in all of life. We need to remember what happened and plan for what will happen. In cases calling for action, we'll need to manage change with the help of the past and the future. This would be especially important in situations where we want to perform our best.

Practical and rational conundrums
Let's consider a surfer riding a wave. How well a surfer can perform will depend on how well she responds to the wave as it is changing moment by moment. On the one hand, it is important for her to be "in the now." A surfer can't respond well if she is

trying to surf a wave that has happened in the past or even if she is trying to surf the wave as it was just a moment ago. To surf the wave as best as she can, she needs to surf this wave as it is now.

On the other hand, the surfer needs to draw upon her previous experience of waves, as well as how this current wave has evolved so far. She needs to be remembering what has happened before in the past and planning how this wave will evolve in the future. This is another example of the practical conundrum. It can seem as if the surfer must balance being now versus the practicality of managing change with past and future in order to surf her best.

Sometimes, though, during moments of peak performance, the surfer might feel a deep sense of connection to all that is going on in her experience right now. She might even feel that what is now is so incredibly rich that it has everything she needs in order to ride the wave, while she more freely and effectively responds "in the flow" of her action. It is as if the practical conundrum—the apparent need for balancing being now versus managing change—has disappeared, but how can she explain this feeling? And how could she practice this feeling so that she could experience more of it?

Historically, it seems that people have experienced being now beyond any need for balance. They may have had this insight after meditating for many years. Or they may have experienced glimpses of this perspective during periods of peak performance. They report an experiential sense that "all we can do is live in this moment," "everything is now," and "each moment is all being," even if there seems to be no consistent explanation for this.

After all, how can *everything* that matters for our lives and our actions—including the past and the future and the flow of change—really be a part of just a fleeting moment, right now? This view can seem inexplicable. Some people have even thought that we must go beyond our rational thinking in order to have such an all-encompassing view of what is now. This is another conundrum about now—a rational conundrum.

As we'll see, it is not surprising that a rational explanation seemed difficult and perhaps even seemingly impossible. People can tend to think of now as now*shape* (i.e., the position, or shape, of things at a moment). Partly because of this, people may think that change is *not* included in now. People can also tend to think that the past and the future in our experience are *not* now, so that we would need to try to block out the past and the future to be now. With such assumptions, we would keep running into both practical and rational conundrums about being now.

General understanding: nowflow

For millennia and into modern times, being "in the now" and "in the flow" have held out promising solutions for human suffering and performance. This book, *Way of Now*, lays out the rational foundation for why and how this is so: Now as nowflow (but not nowshape) is the practical whole. By understanding now as now*flow*, which means that now includes the flow of change, we can resolve both the practical and rational conundrums we've discussed. We'll see how physics further supports nowflow—but not nowshape—as the practical whole of all that can make a difference. This means nowflow includes everything that has interaction potential. It includes change and past-present-future information about change. We'll see how, even as we manage change with past-present-future storylines, those storylines are fully part of what is going on *altogether nowflow*.

With an understanding of now as nowflow, we have a general understanding of what is now that always works in our life experience—such as for meditation, daily life, and the flow state of peak performance— and is also consistent with biology and physics. *There is change going on. There is past-present-future information about change going on. It's all going on altogether now— nowflow.* Understanding nowflow as the practical whole can guide us when we want to be less stressed. It also applies without downside when we need to take action, whatever the action may be.

With this general understanding, we can set aside lingering concerns that "being now" might become impractical, if we take it too far. We can take "being nowflow" as far as we'd like, and it will always only help us. Now as nowflow is a general, practical understanding that we can discover for ourselves—and that can serve as a guide in all that we are and do.

1

What is Now?

What is—and what isn't—in our experience now

Let's say that we're lying in bed. Our bedroom is quiet and peaceful. There's nothing we need to get done right now except get a good night's sleep. This is especially important because we have a big day tomorrow and we'll get through it better if we're rested.

But we can't sleep. We keep thinking about all that needs to happen tomorrow. We may feel as if we are already revved up and may even release stress hormones as if we are already in the midst of tomorrow's challenging events. How could we help ourselves feel the quiet and ease of lying in our bedroom now so we could fall asleep easier?

Forgetting past and future
One possible solution for this would be to try to forget about the future and concentrate on the "here and now." While lying in bed, we could try to focus only on our breathing or on the sights, sounds, and

sensations of lying in our bedroom now. Whenever we notice that we are lost in thought about what will happen tomorrow, we could practice letting the thoughts go.

This is similar to how we might sit in relative peace and quiet during a meditation session. In that kind of situation, we could try not to think about what will happen (or what has happened) as much as possible. Because trying not to think about the future and the past can be helpful to some degree, some people might even view meditation or mindfulness practice as mainly training to do this better in order to be now.

We might consider, though, how well trying to block out the future would work if tomorrow is the most important day of our lives. Could we really just not think about that? Trying to be now by excluding the future could become increasingly difficult and even stressful as we struggle to block out what will happen tomorrow. We might wonder if there is a better way—some solution that could always help us, even in difficult situations.

"Everything now"
Historically, there seems to have been people who had insight into such questions through long meditation practice. Instead of trying to be now by forgetting about the past and the future, they say, "Everything is now."

Let's see how this insight could help us as we lie in bed wanting to fall asleep before an important event the next day. If we're guided by a sense of "everything is now," then we would probably notice the quiet and peace of our bedroom now. We would likely notice our body lying in the bed now, and even our emotions and thoughts that are going on now.

If truly "everything is now," though, what about tomorrow's important event itself? It wouldn't be restful for us if we were feeling this stressful future event as being now, for that could cause us to release stress hormones prematurely. As helpful as it is to notice more of what is going on now, it would also be helpful for us to realize that the future event is completely not now.

Unlike the future event itself, there is something about the future that is happening now, as we lie in bed. We are planning about what will happen tomorrow. This is "the future" of a story about what will happen tomorrow that is going on in our mind now. To manage change, we have storyline information, such as the storylines that let us know what happened yesterday, what is happening, and what will happen tomorrow. Our thinking about tomorrow's event is "the future" part of such a storyline.

As this example shows, "the future" can mean the future event itself. "The future" can also indicate the future part of a storyline, such as the plans in our mind now that we have for what will happen tomorrow. Distinguishing between these *two futures*— one that is completely not now while the other is completely now—can be a start of understanding what is now (and what is not now).

Similarly, we can think of *two pasts*: "the past" of the events themselves that have happened, which are not now, and "the past" of storylines that are going on now about what has happened. This can also help us to feel more free from past stressful events, which are no longer happening now at all, while keeping the lessons of the past event, which are fully a part of now.

All practical is now

As we'll see, "the past" and "the future" of storylines, which are now, can make a practical difference in the sense that they can affect us. While past events are gone and future events are not here yet, "the past" and "the future" of our storylines are affecting us now. This shows the possibility of all that is *practical* is now.

This may still seem surprising because now seems so fleeting. How could now include all that is practical? Can we rationally understand now as the whole of all that can make a practical difference? In this book, we will see how it is change that is "fleeting," while now is always the practical whole, which includes "fleeting" change. This is also consistent with physics.

As we'll see, this general understanding of nowflow fully applies to all our life experience and so connects the "here and now" of meditation to the "flow state" of peak performance.

A first step towards this clarity is to see what is in our experience now—and what isn't—in terms of the two pasts and the two futures. Though we may have some difficulty distinguishing between the two futures as we lie in bed before an important day, there are cases in our everyday life experience where we already distinguish them easily. In these cases, we already see how one is not now at all and the other is completely now, even if we may not consciously realize this. To familiarize ourselves with the two past and two futures, we can start with history books, weather forecasts, and melodies.

2

Information

History books and weather forecasts

Let's say that we are reading a history book about events that happened in ancient cities long ago. As we read the history book, we know that it is a book we're experiencing and not the historical events themselves. We can relate to the book as a resource of available information—happening now—about what has happened.

What would it be like, though, if we weren't clear on this? We might worry that, after opening such a book, we could suddenly find ourselves interacting with an ancient city itself and so feel as if we are partially separating from our experience as it is now. We might even put effort into trying to block out the ancient city as it once was or trying to accept that it is really gone.

In the context of reading a history book, we don't have these kinds of worries, efforts, and confusions. We can perceive how it is the information in the history book—and our reading of it—that is in our experience now. The history book we're holding in our hands right now is not in the past. It is informing us now.

Let's look at another example. We probably don't worry that viewing a weather forecast could cause us to get soaking wet. A weather forecast itself doesn't go pitter-patter on our windows or blow off our hats. As we check a weather forecast, we can relate to the forecast as a resource of available information—happening now—about what will happen.

When we check the forecast, we just want to be informed about what the weather might be like in the future so that we can know whether to pack an umbrella or reschedule an outdoor event. Because we see that the weather forecast is informing us now, we can perceive that the weather forecast—and our checking of it—are not separate from what we are experiencing right now. That's how this information can be available to us and can usefully inform our current actions.

When there is a book or a forecast in front of us, it is easier for us to relate to these sources of information (about what has happened and what will happen) *as happening now*. We perceive how they are part of our current experience as we're looking at them. With other sources of information, though, this may not be so easy for us to realize. That's why it can be helpful to contrast our handling of our personal "histories" and personal "forecasts"—going on in our minds—with our handling of history books and weather forecasts.

Two pasts, two futures

Let's return to the example where we are lying in bed thinking about what might happen tomorrow or what happened yesterday. Perhaps we are regretting an embarrassing thing that we did yesterday or worrying about all that we have to do tomorrow. We can feel as if this information about what has happened or what will happen gets in the way of us more fully being now. We may toss and turn as if struggling in the midst of yesterday's embarrassing incident or tomorrow's many to-dos, instead of feeling the peace and quiet of our bedroom now and getting a good night's rest. How might we help ourselves in this case by seeing what is—and isn't—in our experience as we easily do when relating to history books about ancient cities or forecasts about the weather?

In the case of reading a history book, we naturally don't have to try to block out the ancient city itself or try to accept that it is gone. We just perceive that it is not in our experience now, even though information about it is part of our experience now. In other words, *the past* that is informing us now is fully in our experience now, while *the past* event itself is gone. What if we could more clearly distinguish between these two pasts in the case of lying in bed with regret keeping us awake?

Just as with the ancient city itself, the event itself of yesterday's embarrassing incident is gone. What we did yesterday is not going on now. This is the past that is completely not in our experience anymore. As with reading a history book, what is in our experience now is information about that previous event, thanks to the remembering that is happening now in our mind as we lie in bed. This is the past that is completely in our experience now.

We could also relate to the two futures with the clarity we already have when we look at a weather forecast. Just as with the events of the upcoming rainstorm itself, the events of tomorrow's to-dos are not in our experience yet. That is the future that isn't here yet, and it is not making a practical difference in our experience now because it is not in our experience now at all. What is in our experience now is information about those upcoming events—thanks to the planning that is happening now in our mind. This is the future that we need to manage our lives.

Practically, we need this storyline information about change, such as the storylines that let us know what happened yesterday, what is happening, and what will happen tomorrow. We may also feel that the past of a storyline (about what happened yesterday) and the future of a storyline (about what will happen tomorrow) can tend to interfere in our ability to feel more fully now. We've seen, though, that the past

and future of a storyline are actually in our experience now, just as reading a history book or looking
at a weather forecast is in our experience now and
informing us now.

What if, instead of feeling as if the past and the future
get in the way of our current experience, we could
naturally feel how the past and the future of our
storylines inform and contribute to our current experience now? To explore this possibility, we can put on
some music and listen.

3

Storylines

Feeling "in the flow" of music

How do we hear and recognize our own name? Our ears just register whatever sound vibrations are interacting with them. When someone calls our name, there are a series of sound vibrations that happen and then are gone—one after another. If someone says the name Ella, for example, our mind is remembering the "El" sound even as it hears the "la" sound so we can hear that name.

As another example, let's say that we are listening to some live music. The musicians are just playing the notes they are playing. Our eardrum is just vibrating with whatever sound vibrations that it is interacting with at a moment. Yet we are hearing a melody as a series of notes. If we are listening to the opening phrase of Beethoven's *5th Symphony*, our mind is remembering the three previously repeated notes—"dah, dah, dah"— even as it registers the final "dum" sound.

To better recognize the role that remembering plays
in our current experience of sound, it can be helpful
to reflect on what our experience might be like if we
weren't remembering the previous sounds. What
would it be like to listen to the "Happy Birthday"
song without remembering any previous notes? We'd
basically just hear the "hap-" note and then the "-py"
note. When hearing the "-py" note, we'd have no
sense of the previous note that came before it. Only
isolated blips of sound would be in our experience.

Without our remembering of the previous note, we
also couldn't know whether the current note was
higher or lower in pitch than the sound before it. We
wouldn't know if it was louder or softer. We wouldn't
have a storyline about how the music has changed.
There'd be no sense of rhythm or melody. That would
be quite unlike what we actually experience, which
shows how our mind must be remembering the
previous sounds in order to experience the melody of
"Happy Birthday" as we do.

This remembering can feel different, though, than our
remembering of the events of yesterday. Even though
our experience of melody involves remembering what
has happened, we don't tend to feel that the past of
the melody takes away from what is happening now.
Instead, we usually feel that the previous notes in the
melody add to our current enjoyment of the note we
are hearing. We naturally feel how this information

about what has happened is a part of our current experience—now—of the melody and music.

"Past" and "future" now

Let's see this in terms of our storylines about change. As we listen, we have a storyline about the sounds and their changes: the sound *was* like that (past) and it *is* like this (present). With our remembering and current hearing of sound, we can experience a melodic storyline. We might also have some plans or predictions for what the sound will be, such as anticipating the upcoming notes or rhythm: the sound *will be* like that (future).

We can experience a melody because of the past and the present of our storyline about the changing sounds, yet, instead of feeling as if the past of our melodic storyline somehow gets in the way of our experience right now, we naturally feel how it is part of our experience of the music right now. We can feel how the past of our melodic storyline is also a part of what is happening in our experience altogether now.

In other words, when we listen to music, we correctly process this available information about what has happened in the music as part of what is happening now in our experience as we listen. We can enjoy the richness of contrasts, patterns, and differences in how the sound has changed or will change without feeling as if this experience of change partially separates us from now.

"Flow" now

While we listen to music, we don't tend to feel as if our remembering or anticipating of changes in sounds gets in the way of our current listening experience. Instead, we may feel "in the flow" of the change of sounds as we listen now. Even without realizing that these melodic storylines are going on now in our mind, we tend to process the change—the flow—of listening to music as part of all that we are experiencing right now.

This opens up an interesting possibility. Perhaps we could help ourselves to process other storylines about change more correctly, as we already naturally do while enjoying a melody. What if we could feel "in the flow" of our current experience now, even as we are remembering what happened yesterday or planning for what will happen tomorrow—or even if we are running late to an important meeting?

4

Trouble

Running late and the apparent tradeoff

Let's say we're running late to an important meeting. We might be so caught up in stressful thoughts about what will happen that we hardly see where we are going as we hurry along the sidewalk. While in this state of distraction, we might even begin to cross a street without clearly assessing the traffic around us. Perhaps it's the honk of a horn that wakes us up to the fact that a car is coming towards us. We jump back onto the curb with our heart racing. How did that just happen? How is it that we could be so blinded by worry and stress about the future that we would endanger our life right now in an effort to get to a meeting?

Although this is a rather dramatic example, it demonstrates how we sometimes feel—and also act—as if we can partially separate from what is going on now. In the case of getting to the meeting, we could feel so caught up in the future of arriving late that we act

as if we've partially disconnected from being now.
We don't even notice and respond to such important
current goings-on as an oncoming car.

Tradeoff: now vs. the future

As we are hurrying to our meeting, we have a
storyline about change: I *was* back there, I *am* here, and
I *will be* there. This storyline has a past, present, and
future. We are remembering where we were. We are
seeing where we are now. We are planning for where
we will be.

Because the future of getting to the meeting is so
important to us (yet can seem separate from what's
going on now), we might feel and act as if the future of
getting to the meeting is partially separating us from
what is happening now. As we hurry to get to our
meeting, it's as if we can't fully take care of both what
will happen in the future and what's going on now.
It's as if there is some fundamental tradeoff.

This sense of a fundamental separation or tradeoff
between now vs. "the future" of getting to the meeting
can force us to make strangely incorrect prioritiza-
tions. It can cause us to give so little care and attention
to crossing the street now that we fail to notice an
oncoming car. After we step back on the curb, we
might try to find a better balance between now vs.
"the future." We might stand for a minute while
taking some deep breaths and telling ourselves, "If I'm
late, I'm late. I need to accept that."

Case by case, situation by situation, we might try to figure out a better practical balance between taking care of now and the future. Perhaps without even realizing it, we may believe that this tradeoff is fundamentally just the way things work so that we have to prioritize one over the other: now *or* the future. But is this actually the way things work?

Altogether solution

What if we were able to more clearly relate to our own planning as something that is going on now? After all, our plans about getting to the meeting have information about what will happen, but they aren't really somehow less now than other parts of our experience.

We've seen how we can check a weather forecast without feeling as if we're partially separating from now. In that situation, we distinguish between the future that is now (and can make a practical difference in our experience by informing us now) and the future weather that isn't here yet. We can relate to available information in a forecast about what will happen as something that is fully happening in our experience now.

We've also seen how we can experience a melody thanks to past-present-future storyline information about how the sound was, is, and will be, while feeling how all of this is included in our experience of the music now. If we are anticipating the next notes of

the "Happy Birthday" song, we naturally feel that is
included in our current experience of the song, instead
of feeling as if that anticipation must take away from
our current experience.

The future of our personal storyline—*I will be late to
the meeting*— is what we are anticipating in our mind
now. As we hurry to cross the street, our anticipation
of *I will be late to the meeting* and our current perception
of *I am here at the crosswalk* are the future and the
present of a storyline that is going on in our mind
right now. There isn't some fundamental separation or
tradeoff we have to make between the future and the
present of this storyline, because both are happening
together—now—in our mind.

With this clarity about what is in our experience
now, we could feel more connected to whatever is
happening, which includes planning to get to the
meeting *and* seeing the oncoming traffic. Our planning
is, after all, informing our current actions now. So,
too, is our remembering. So, too, is our seeing what's
going on around us. By having clearer perception of
all that is in our experience *now*, we could make better
decisions moment by moment in our actions. This is a
solution to our troubles that could always help us.

Better info, better action

To get to our meeting while being "in the now," we
don't have to give up on the future outcome that

we want or partially block out our anticipating and planning for it. The future that is making a practical difference is fully in our experience now. By realizing this, we could relate to our own planning more as we would relate to a weather forecast or upcoming notes in a melody. We could feel "in the flow" of our current experience of change now, which includes both our seeing that I *am* here and our planning for I *will* be there.

With this sense of being "in the flow" of our action now, we could even come up with better routes and more efficiently navigate our way through the car and pedestrian traffic. By having more clarity about all that is going on now, we could take better care of all the practical aspects of our action. We could get to the meeting place on time, if that were possible. Whatever might happen next, we'd be at our most ready to handle it. As we enter the meeting room, we'd already be "in the flow" of handling all that is happening moment by moment as well as we could.

Even as we respond and take action, we could feel better—more fully alive yet at peace. We wouldn't have to feel scattered, stressed, and harried by our efforts to get there. It can sound almost too good to be true because there is a tendency to feel as if we must make a fundamental tradeoff between managing change with past-present-future and fully being now. We have seen, though, how managing change with past-present-future is fully part of now. This is something we can understand generally and can come to more clearly perceive so that we can have better action.

5

Altogether Now

The past and the future

As children watch clouds, they may point out the shapes that the clouds are making. Perhaps they say, "That cloud looks like a turtle." Then a little while later, the cloud doesn't look so much like a turtle anymore.

If we look for the turtle-shaped cloud in the sky, we can't find it. It's just not there anymore—it's gone. It has changed into something else. Perhaps the cloud now looks more like a buffalo. Yet there is still something about that turtle-shaped cloud in our experience. What is in our experience now is the past of our storyline about the cloud: It used to look like a turtle (past), and now it looks more like a buffalo (present).

As we've seen, what can be confusing is that the past of our storyline about the cloud is actually in our experience now. It is a memory happening now in our mind. While the turtle-shaped cloud itself is not now anymore, the memory of it is informing us now and making a practical difference now as the past of that storyline.

Let's see this in another basic example. As we go to catch a moving ball, what is actually in our experience and making a practical difference for our action? If we point and say, "The ball *was* there," there is no ball in the place where we are pointing. It's moved elsewhere. Also, if we point and say, "The ball will be there," there isn't a ball where we are pointing. It's just not there yet.

The ball is not where it used to be in the past or where it will be in the future. What's happening now in terms of the ball is just *the moving ball is here now*. Yet, would we want to attempt to catch a ball without the past and the future? When a player catches a fly ball in baseball, he runs in a direction based on a prediction for where the ball will be. As the player continues to get more information about the trajectory that the ball has taken so far, he keeps updating his plans for where the ball is heading so he can move to where he needs to be in order to catch it. The past and the future of the player's storyline about the ball are allowing him to catch the ball.

If we're playing catch, we would need the past of a storyline, which is going on in our mind now as a memory, about where the ball used to be. We would

need the future of a storyline, which is happening in
our mind now as a plan, about where the ball will be.
The past and the future of our storylines about change
are in our experience now, informing us now, and
making a practical difference now.

Fully now, fully practical

Before taking a closer look at our experience, we
may tend to think that the past and the future in our
experience are *not* now. If someone said, "The past
and future are now," we may think that doesn't make
much sense. As we've seen, it can be puzzling because
there are two pasts and two futures, but we don't
always distinguish between the two.

We have taken a closer look at our own experience,
though. With the help of history books, weather forecasts, and melodies, we've seen how the past and the
future of past-present-future storylines about change
are fully in our experience now. Even though it may be
harder for us to feel in other cases, we can know that
this understanding fully applies to all of our experience: our past-present-future storylines about change
are always completely now.

Without distinguishing between the two pasts and two
futures, though, it wouldn't make sense to say that
"the past" and "the future" are now. For example, the
future event itself of being late is not happening now,
and it wouldn't help us get to the meeting if we were
feeling that stressful event as now.

The past events and the future upcoming events themselves are gone or not here yet. They don't currently have a practical influence on us at all and are *completely* not now, so they cannot separate us from now. On the other hand, the past and the future of our storylines that are influencing us are *completely* now, so they cannot separate us from now either.

As we've seen, it's the past and the future of our storylines, which are fully now, that can make a practical difference in our experience. Because past-present-future storylines about change are included in now, being now is not a matter of excluding the past and the future of our storylines. Now includes all available storyline information about how things *used to be* (past), how things *are* (present), and how things *will be* (future), so we can fully be now without practical downsides. This is how we can take "being now" as far as we would like without practical conundrums.

Even while practically using this understanding of fully being now, one might still wonder how now could be the practical whole that includes change. To resolve this rational conundrum, we would need a more general understanding of now. In the next chapter, a general, rational explanation will be presented on how now includes all that can make a practical difference, including change.

6

Nowflow

Change included

In various traditions and cultures, people have long reflected on the experience of change. In ancient Greece, an early philosopher wrote, "Ever changing water flows over those stepping into the same river." In ancient China, people would consult *I Ching*, or *Book of Changes*. Long ago in India, a prince left his palace and saw sickness, old age, and death for the first time. He later became known as the Awakened One, or Buddha, and taught on the truth of impermanence.

There are things that aren't now as they used to be in the past. There are things that aren't going to be in the future as they are now. This is one of the most basic insights we can reflect on: There is change.

As much as change is part of our experience, though, we've seen how we can have some confusion about how we experience it. We can tend to feel as if we are separating from now as we experience change. This feeling may be related to how we tend to think of now as nowshape.

Nowflow, not nowshape

If one is thinking about now as now*shape* (i.e., the position, or shape, of things at a moment), then the flow of change would not be included in nowshape. Let's see this in a simple example of a thrown ball. The nowshape of a moving ball would not include that the ball is mov*ing*—the ball's velocity.

In terms of now as nowshape, these two different situations would be indistinguishable: a ball at some position that is moving very fast horizontally and a ball at the same position that is moving very slowly vertically. Given our experience of moving balls, though, we know that the ball's velocity makes a practical difference.

In those two situations, we would head to different places to catch the ball depending on how the ball is moving. In other words, once we have a sense of the flow of the ball now, we also have a sense of the ball's storyline trajectory. This reaffirms that now can include all available storyline information, as we've already seen, but only if now includes the flow of change.

Once the flow of change is included in now, then now also includes all available past-present-future information about change. This is how we can rationally understand now, which includes the flow of change, as the whole of all that can make a practical difference. We can use the word "nowflow" as a reminder that now includes the flow of change.

As we'll see in a later chapter, this is also consistent with physics. Physics can quantitatively model and reaffirm that nowflow, which includes velocity, includes all available past-present-future storyline information.

Fleeting flow of change now

Even with this rational understanding, it may still feel somewhat surprising that now could be the practical whole. After all, now may tend to seem so fleeting, as if it's always slipping away from us. If we step into a flowing river, the water is not now as it was one moment ago and will not be as it is now in the next moment. It can be hard to imagine how something "so fleeting" as now could encompass so much as to be practically all-encompassing.

As an aid to open our minds, we could consider a world in which there is no change. In that case, now would remain the same and so would not seem to be fleeting. This can help us to see how it is the flow of change that is fleeting, while now is always the practical whole, which includes "fleeting" change and also our perception of "fleeting" change, as described below.

Chang*ed* and chang*ing*—now

We have the experience of things changing now, such as when we are standing in a flow*ing* river, observing a mov*ing* ball, or listening to a ris*ing* note. It can be helpful to see how even our perception of the "fleeting" flow of change is also fully included in now.

To see this, let's first look at how our storylines can allow us to experience that something has chang*ed*. For example, by remembering where a ball used to be (past), we can compare it with our seeing of where the ball is (present). That's one way we can know the ball has mov*ed*. Or, by remembering how a sound used to be (past) and comparing it with our hearing of the current sound (present), we can experience that the sound has chang*ed*. These are examples of how the past and the present in our storylines let us have the experience that something has chang*ed*. Since past-present-future storylines are now, this shows that our perception of how something has chang*ed* is also part of now.

We can also have storylines with shorter increments between the past and the present. With increasingly shorter increments as we watch a moving ball, we can experience that the ball is mov*ing* now. Similarly, with increasingly shorter increments between the past and the present in our storyline as we listen to music, we can experience how a note is chang*ing*. These are examples of how the past and the present in our subconscious storylines can let us have the experience that something is chang*ing*. In this way, we can see how our storylines, which are now, can also contain our feeling of the flow of change.

In other words, our experience of how a cloud changed (because it was in a shape of a turtle a few moments ago and is in the shape of a buffalo now) is included in nowflow. Our experience of how a cloud is chang*ing* now is also included in nowflow. All our available information about how things have changed and are changing is included in nowflow.

Nowflow: practical whole

This is a rational understanding that we can fully apply without any downsides: *There's change going on. There's information about change going on. It's all going on altogether now — nowflow.* In this way, all that can make a practical difference is part of nowflow without conundrums or contradictions.

After all, we experience change. Change makes a practical difference. It would be a contradiction to think that nowshape, which doesn't include change, could be practically all-encompassing. Historically, this could be a reason why the experiential sense of "everything is now" seemed difficult to explain rationally. Because of this rational conundrum, it might have even seemed necessary to go beyond rational thinking in order to have a practically all-encompassing view of now.

As we've seen, though, we can rationally understand
nowflow as the practical whole. There are things
that aren't as they used to be and that won't stay as
they are now. There is change. Yet we don't have to
experience change through some confusion, as if we
are partially separating from now as we experience
change. We can understand and more clearly perceive
that now—nowflow—includes the flow of change and
all available information about change.

Nowflow would always work as a way to clearly
distinguish what is in our experience (and making a
practical difference) and what isn't because nowflow
is the practical whole. In the next chapter, we'll begin
to apply this nowflow understanding to see how it can
help us as we are meditating, going about our daily
lives, and engaging in peak performance.

7

Life Experience

How nowflow works for meditation,
peak performance, and daily life

In our lives, we can find ourselves in widely different situations. Peak performance in sports or the arts, for example, may require us to do difficult feats. Meditation, by contrast, might seem to require periods without demands or pressure to get something done. To see how we could apply nowflow understanding in various situations, we'll start by looking at how nowflow works in both peak performance and meditation. We'll find that we don't need one way of being now for when we want to be less stressed and another for when we want to take action. This can help us to see how it is possible to generally apply nowflow understanding—without tradeoffs and exceptions—in all of life experience.

Peak performance—"doing"
When people have a glimpse of being "in the flow" during peak performances, it can feel like a dramatic shift in their experience. Even if they are doing

something difficult, they may feel that their action just "flows." Yet how is it that everything feels easier as it is happening—as if it just flows—while the performer is doing something quite difficult and getting such optimal results? It can seem puzzling, maybe even mysterious.

Would the flow state seem so mysterious, though, in light of an understanding of now as nowflow? In moments of peak performance, a surfer may feel how the wave, her body, and even her mental activity of remembering and planning are happening *altogether nowflow*. With this clarity of perception, she would have fuller awareness of all that contributes to her action as being "in the flow" of what is going on now.

For example, the surfer wouldn't feel a sense of fundamental tradeoff between planning for an upcoming move she will do and perceiving how the wave is changing now. Instead, she could feel how all of her experience and all of her action are in the flow of the practical whole of nowflow. As a result, she could respond more freely and effectively to all that makes a practical difference in her action. She may feel that her action just flows even as she surfs at her best.

Although the experience of feeling "in the flow" may seem incredible, we're seeing how it could arise quite naturally. *There's change going on. There's information about change going on. It's all going on altogether now—*

nowflow. Everything that makes a practical difference in the surfer's action is included in nowflow.

When the surfer has clearer perception of how her experience of change is fully included in *altogether nowflow,* she'll tend to feel more in the flow of change and also handle the flow of change better for her action. This can give us an understanding of reported experiences of the flow state, including traditional accounts in classic texts. With a general understanding of nowflow, we could also see various ways of practicing for the flow state. One way we can have clearer perception of nowflow is through the practice of meditation.

Meditation—"being"

In meditation practices, people often set aside periods when there is not any specific demand to do something. They might minimize the distractions in their environment for a while and practice by being more mindful of their breathing as they sit in a quiet room. This can seem quite different than the situation of the surfer riding a difficult wave. Let's see, though, how such a practice could also help the surfer to have clearer perception of *altogether nowflow,* which would fully apply even in the midst of difficult actions.

During a session, a meditator might practice by following these common meditation instructions: to observe her own breathing and let the thoughts go when she notices that they have distracted her from this moment-by-moment awareness of her breath. Gradually through practice, her mind can become less noisy and scattered so that she can feel the moment-by-moment flow of her breathing more clearly, instead of feeling lost in mental chatter about what has happened, what should be happening, or what will happen.

This is sometimes called "calm-abiding," or samatha, in meditation practice. As she continues to practice, the meditator might feel how her mind quiets down so that she can increasingly be mindful of her body, her senses, and also her emotions and thoughts. Through this clearer perception of her own experience, the meditator can have insight, or vipassana, into the nature of her experience.

We can see what insights this practice might lead to in light of nowflow understanding. For example, when the meditator notices that she's lost in thought about what happened in the past or what will happen in the future, she is giving herself the opportunity to have a key insight into her experience: she can notice how the past and the future in her experience are memories and plans *going on now* in her mind. During these periods of quiet observation, she can more easily discover her thinking as *thinking that is happening now* in her mind.

Again and again, she can observe how the past and
the future of her storylines about change are actually
happening in her experience right now. Because she is
more closely observing her experience, the meditator
could have a dawning insight that the past and the
future of her storylines don't actually separate her
from being now. Though she may sometimes feel as
if her thinking "takes her away" from being now, she
can gradually begin to relate to memories and plans as
going on now along with all aspects of her experience
that are happening altogether now. *There's change going
on. There's information about change going on. It's all going
on altogether now — nowflow.*

With this view of meditation practice, we wouldn't be
trying to get rid of anything or to exclude anything
from our experience. For example, we wouldn't be
trying to block out the past and the future of our
storylines in order to try to be now. After all, we
would need the past and the future to manage our
actions once we're off the meditation cushion.

Instead, the practice would enable us to have less
illusion that we are ever separating from now. We
could let ourselves perceive our experience—and
the way it is always *altogether nowflow*—more clearly.
Though we might first discover this in meditation
sessions without external distractions and demands,
the clearer perception of *altogether nowflow* can always
be helpful, whatever the situation. With this approach,

a meditation practice can fully carry over into our greatest challenges, as well as the demands and to-dos of our daily lives.

Living in the now—being and doing

In the midst of daily life, we can often feel caught up in the past or the future of our storylines as we try to bring about the outcomes we want and to do the things we need to get done. This can make us feel as if we are not fully now. We might feel so caught up in the future of getting to a meeting, for example, that we feel partially disconnected from what is going on now. We might not even notice an oncoming car as we cross the street.

What would it be like, though, if we could more readily recognize when we're feeling caught up in the future of our storylines? With practice, we could notice that the future of our storyline about getting to the meeting is actually a plan in our experience right now. As we hurry to our meeting, we could find ourselves practicing meditation right in the midst of the demands of daily life by observing and reminding ourselves how the future of our storyline is "here and now," too. With that clarity of perception, we could feel how our plans for the future are current information going on now so they don't have to fundamentally interfere with other information, such as seeing an oncoming car.

With this fullness of perception, we could be more aware and responsive to all that is contributing to our action now: our storylines, our mental activity, our emotions, and our body, as well as the cars and pedestrians around us. We could feel more in the flow of change, even as we do all that we can to get to our meeting on time. We might even experience peak performance in our action of getting to our meeting.

This is an example of how daily life can be a meditation and a peak performance. We wouldn't need to feel as if there is a divide between an elusive flow state of peak performance on the one hand and our everyday state of handling more mundane changes in our lives on the other hand. We wouldn't need to associate meditation with "just being," while the rest of our life is filled with things we need "to do." Whatever we are doing and being, it's all happening altogether nowflow. *There's change going on. There's information about change going on. It's all going on altogether now—nowflow.*

8

Biological Function

Altogether nowflow in biological systems

In this chapter, we'll see how an understanding of nowflow also applies to basic biological processes by looking at patterns of change in living beings. Before looking at biological processes, though, let's first consider a pattern of change in a river and a factory.

In the river, there is water that first goes around a rock, then over a waterfall, and then into an eddy. We can look at this pattern and see that the same drop of water cannot be going around the rock *and* be going into the eddy at the same moment. That's not happening together now.

We can also see that all of the drops of water in the river are all flowing altogether now. Some drops of water are flowing around the rock now, while some are flowing over the waterfall now and other drops of water are flowing into the eddy now. In this broader view, we see that whatever is happening in the river is happening altogether now.

In a factory, there could be an assembly line where the first stage of the process is the cutting of a toy. At the second stage of the process, the toy is glued together, and then in the final stage the toy is painted. Again, we can see how, for any one toy, that pattern of change happens in a sequence so that one specific toy is not at the first stage and the last stage in the same moment.

Just as with the flowing river, if we step back and see the broader picture of the working assembly line, we would also see how all of those three stages are going on now simultaneously. If we take an even broader view, we could also see that the whole working toy factory is going on *altogether nowflow*.

Can't be now?

As with the pattern of change in a flowing river or a running assembly line, biological function involves patterns of change that can happen repeatedly in a certain order or sequence. One example of this is how we put food in our mouth before it gets to our stomach. The same bite of food isn't in our mouth and in our stomach at the same moment. There is a process with stages so that, when the bite of food is in our stomach, the chewing of that food in our mouth has happened in the past.

Our perception is also a process with stages. For us to hear what we hear right now, there were sound waves that hit our eardrum a few milliseconds ago.

That stimulus was turned into a nerve signal, which traveled up our auditory nerve to our brain, and then we hear the sound. If we are seeing a moving ball, we know that light had to travel from the ball, hit our eyes, be translated into signals that traveled up our optic nerve, and then were processed by our brain so that we see what we see: *the ball is here.*

In other words, when we are seeing *the ball is here,* this is because light came from the ball when it was in that position in the past. This brings us to one of the apparent conflicts that can come up about "being now." There are people with a background in biology who argue that we can't really "be now" because our perception of seeing and hearing, for example, are due to a process that takes a few milliseconds. It might seem like a contradiction: What we see right now—*the ball is here now*—actually comes from light that traveled from the ball when it was there in the recent past. But do the stages of our perception have to mean that we cannot "be now"?

Whole view

We can look at this question first in terms of the assembly line in the factory. When we have a finished toy, the cutting of that toy happened in the past, but this wouldn't mean that the finished toy cannot be now. In a broader view, we can see that the finished toy, the running assembly line, and the whole working factory are all part of now.

Similarly, when we see *the ball is here*, the light came from the ball in that position in the past, but this wouldn't mean that our seeing isn't happening now. The "whole factory" of our body and mind, the "assembly line" process of our perception, and the "end product" of our seeing are all continuously happening altogether now. *There's change going on. There's information about change going on. It's all going on altogether now — nowflow.*

Knowledge about biological processes, such as the process of our perception, helps us to see in greater detail how our biological functioning happens. As we've seen, this knowledge is consistent with how our biological functioning is always part of all that's going on altogether nowflow. In the next chapter, we'll see how nowflow understanding—where change and all available change information are included in now—is also consistent with physics.

9

Physics

Consistent with change and all available
information in nowflow

We have seen that now can be the practical whole of
all that makes a difference—if we understand now as
nowflow. This is because nowflow includes change
and all available information about change. In this
chapter, we'll see how this understanding is also
consistent with physics. As we'll see, one now*shape*
moment is very tiny compared to the rest of a storyline
about change. It's almost insignificant. By contrast,
now*flow* is in principle all-encompassing. It includes
all of the available storyline information about change
in physics.

Almost insignificant to all-encompassing
To see this in an example, we can contrast nowshape
and nowflow in the case of a simple physics problem
about a moving ball. Let's say that we are looking at
a graph that plots where the ball is at each moment
over the trajectory of a moving ball. We then decide
that we just want to look at only one moment. Perhaps

we even erase all the other moments from the graph so that we're just left with one point: the position of the ball at a moment. What can we know about the storyline of the ball's trajectory just by looking at that one point?

With only the position of the ball at a moment, we wouldn't know whether the ball is moving in a fast, horizontal line or whether the ball is slowly moving straight up. Even if we "plug in" the position of the ball at a moment into the Newtonian physics equations for motion, we won't be able to solve for the ball's trajectory.

From this example, we can see how the position of the ball at one moment is not enough to have a storyline about the ball's trajectory. The nowshape description of *the ball is here at this position* is missing practical information about how the ball is moving, as well as how the ball has moved or will move. In other words, the position of the ball at a moment is almost insignificant compared to all the information we could have about where the ball has been and where it is going.

Let's contrast this with a nowflow description of *the ball is here at this position and is moving with this velocity* at one moment. We can return to the plot of the arcing trajectory of the moving ball and decide again that we just want to look at only one moment on the graph. In contrast, though, to what we did before, let's also keep in mind that the ball has a velocity at that moment. We might picture the velocity as an arrow, indicating the ball's speed and direction of movement at that moment.

At first, it might look as if the information available to us in this case is also insignificant compared to all the information of the ball's trajectory. We have just two values—the position and velocity at a moment— compared to all the many values that were plotted out before as a storyline of the ball's arcing movement.

Even without formal physics, though, we can know from our own experience that we have some information about where the ball has been and where the ball is going in this case. Based on our own experience of how objects move under earth's gravity, we'd know that a ball moving in a fast, horizontal line is going to make a long, thin arcing trajectory. We'd know that a ball moving straight up quite slowly is about to fall back down. Given the position and the velocity of the ball at a moment, we can have a sense of the storyline for the ball's trajectory.

With Newtonian physics equations, we can have a more accurate storyline for the ball's trajectory by plugging in the position and velocity of the ball at a moment into these equations. We can solve these equations so that we get numbers for the ball all through its arcing trajectory. This confirms our experience that there is much more information in nowflow than nowshape.

From this example of a simple physics problem, we can see that just the ball's position at a moment is not enough to encompass all that is practical, including all available information about the moving ball. By contrast, the position and the velocity of the ball at one moment is enough to be practically all-encompassing, including all the storyline information available in physics about where the ball has been and where it is going.

General physics

Even though we have only contrasted nowshape and nowflow in a basic example of Newtonian physics, this applies generally in physics. The equations that let us solve for the trajectory of the moving ball in this example are second order differential equations, which require two initial conditions. In our simple example, we saw that the two initial conditions of position and velocity at a moment are enough to solve for the storyline of the ball's movement. We also saw that just the one initial condition (i.e., position at a moment) isn't enough for this type of equation to be solvable.

In more complex cases of Newtonian physics and even Einstein's relativity and quantum mechanics, the corresponding equations are also second order

differential equations as is the case with our simple
Newtonian physics example. This lets us know that
one moment as position and velocity is enough in
principle for having all the available storyline information in our physics problem, however complex a
problem or however general our physics.

In this way, an understanding of physics is consistent
with and even further clarifies that now as nowflow—
but not as nowshape—is the practical whole of all
that can make a difference. *Change is an inherent part
of now—nowflow. All available information about change
is included in nowflow. Everything that can make a practical difference is a part of the practical whole of nowflow.*
With this understanding, now is still just now—this
moment—but it is not so insignificant as would be the
case with nowshape. Now as nowflow encompasses
all that is significant practically, and we can understand this rationally and generally in a way that is
consistent with science.

10

Clarity

Seeing through the illusion of separation

We have seen how nowflow understanding works for physics, for biology, and for life experience—whether in daily life, meditation, or peak performance. Nowflow is the practical whole of all that can make a difference, including change. We experience change and yet all of our experience is happening altogether now—nowflow. In this way, we can rationally understand that we are never actually separating from altogether nowflow, even while we might feel and act as if we are.

Two pasts: gone past and storyline past

Let's see how we could help remind ourselves that we are fully now, even if we may be feeling and acting as if we're not. For example, let's say that we've just missed a shot while playing a basketball game. As we run back to defend our basketball hoop, we might feel regret or even embarrassment for having missed the shot. Perhaps we long for a do-over. This can make us feel stuck in the past event, which is over and gone, instead of being able to play more fully "in the flow" of the game that's happening now.

A teammate might remind us, "You can't do anything about it. It's the *gone past*." By saying that the missed shot is the *gone past*, the teammate is helping us to see more clearly what isn't in our experience. The event of missing the shot itself is over—gone. What is in our experience is our *storyline past* about missing the shot. That is a memory that's going on in our mind now.

Let's see how this clarity about the two pasts—the *gone past* and the *storyline past*—can help us continue to play at our best, instead of feeling partially stuck "in the past" of missing our shot. Perhaps we adjust our shot or anticipate a defender's move based on previous experience, even while we respond in the moment to the game that's continuing to unfold around us, playing as best we can right now. We can feel how all that is practical for our action is in the flow of altogether nowflow: the *storyline past* is informing us now, while the event of the *gone past* is completely gone from our experience now. With this clarity about what is—and what isn't—in our experience now, it can be easier to learn from our past mistakes and move on.

Two futures: not-here future and storyline future

Let's also see how we could remind ourselves that the future in our experience is not really separating us from now. Let's say we're a stressed-out student who is worried about an upcoming test. As our mind stays caught up in thoughts about whether we will succeed or fail, we may feel somewhat separated from now and "thrown into the future" of what could happen. Our body might even release stress hormones as if we were already taking the important test or receiving a poor grade. This can make it harder for us to just focus on learning as much as we can.

A teacher might give us this advice, "The test itself and how you will do on it is the *not-here future*." In other words, the future event itself of taking the test or getting the grade is *not-here*—it's not yet in our experience now. By saying that the result of the test is the *not-here future*, the teacher is helping us to see more clearly what isn't in our experience. That upcoming event is just not part of our experience now. What is in our experience now is our *storyline future* about that upcoming event. That is fully a part of what is happening now because it is a plan happening now in our mind.

With this clarity about what is—and what isn't—in our experience now, the future wouldn't seem to separate us from our experience now. The *not-here future* event is completely not here—it's not now at all. The *storyline future* is completely here—it is fully now in our experience. By realizing that all of our experience is happening altogether right now, we can prepare for our upcoming test without feeling as if the future of our test is getting in the way of us more fully being now. Right now, moment by moment, we can take care of what we can to ensure the best outcome for our test, which includes our planning and anticipating for the test.

Past, present, future: rock, paper, scissors

As simple as this is, it can be helpful to use a concrete example to demonstrate to ourselves what is in our experience now—and what isn't. The childhood hand game of rock, paper, scissors is a series of three hand gestures. First we make our hand into a fist for rock. Then we flatten it out so that the palm is open for paper. Then we leave only our index and middle finger extended for scissors. We'll look at this sequence of rock, paper, and scissors in terms of the past, present, and future. When our hand is paper (present) in this sequence, then our hand used to be rock (past) and will be scissors (future).

When our hand is paper, let's look for our hand itself as rock. If we do this, we see how our hand itself is no longer rock at all because our hand is paper now. Our hand itself as rock is the *gone past*. We can also see how our hand itself is not scissors yet. Our hand itself as scissors is the *not-here future*.

So what is the past and the future in our experience now as we play this childhood hand game of rock, paper, scissors? While our hand is at paper, we have a memory going on in our mind now about how our hand used to be rock. This is the *storyline past*. We also have a plan going on in our mind now about how our hand will be scissors. This is the *storyline future*.

From this simple hand-game exercise, we can see that our hand is changing and we are experiencing that change, yet we are not separating from now. There is our changing hand itself. There is our past-present-future storyline information going on in our mind about our hand so that we know it used to be rock, is paper, and will be scissors. It's all happening together—now. It's all a part of nowflow.

All practical now: past-present-future

Perhaps we made a mistake yesterday. The event itself that happened to us yesterday is gone. We aren't in those previous circumstances, making that previous mistake anymore. Just as we did when we looked for the *gone past* of our hand itself as rock, we can take a moment and really see that the event itself of yesterday's mistake is just not now. It's over—done and *gone*.

Perhaps tomorrow we have something coming up that we are dreading or that we feel pressure to do well. The event itself that might happen to us tomorrow

isn't here yet. We aren't in those upcoming circumstances, doing that task or performance. Just as we
did when we looked for the *not-here future* of our hand
itself as scissors, we can actually look for the event
itself that will happen tomorrow and find that it's just
not here.

Just as in the hand game, we need to look to our mind
to find the past and the future in our experience as the
storyline past and the *storyline future*. It's the past and
the future of our past-present-future storyline about
change that are affecting us now and are making a
practical difference for us now.

We have this *storyline past* and *storyline future* information that is happening altogether now as nowflow,
while the *gone past* and *not-here future* events themselves are not now in our experience at all. However
much we might regret a missed opportunity or be
anxious about an upcoming one, we can never actually separate from altogether nowflow, which fully
includes the flow of change. Would we experience as
much stressful emotion if we had this clarity about
what's making a difference in our experience—and
what is just not?

11

Wisdom through the Ages

Applying nowflow to traditional sayings

Change can be hard. When the Indian prince Siddhartha (who later became known as the Buddha) reflected on illness, old age, and death, he realized that people are not only suffering because of their illness that is happening now. There is additional suffering because the ill person once was healthy. The elderly person was once young. Before someone dear to us passes away, they were alive and with us. We suffer additionally because we compare what is to what used to be. Perhaps things used to be better in the past and now they are worse.

We can tend to have stressful emotions about resisting change that goes from better to worse or craving change that goes from worse to better. How could nowflow understanding help us to suffer less from this kind of stress? For thousands of years, people have found emotional solace and helpful life advice in the traditional sayings quoted below. We can look at these sayings in light of our understanding of nowflow as the practical whole, which includes our experience of change. As an exercise in applying nowflow understanding, we can see how each of these quotes could help us to let go of some aspect of the illusion that we are somehow separating from now as we experience and manage change.

Fighting a noble battle

In the Hindu scripture of the *Bhagavad Gita*, Lord Krishna advises a warrior on how to have the best outcome in a noble fight. Lord Krishna says to the warrior: "To action alone hast thou a right and never at all to its fruits."

To see how we might apply this advice in an example, let's say that a teacher advises a student not to worry about the "fruits," or results, of an upcoming test. At first the student might be taken aback by this advice: "Isn't it important to do well? Is the teacher telling me not to care about the test?" Such questions highlight the potential for confusion that could cause the student to lapse into passivity rather than achieve the best possible outcome on the test.

To help the student avoid this confusion, we could apply nowflow understanding to the teacher's advice. The "fruits" of the future outcomes themselves are just not here yet. We can't grasp them now. We can't guarantee them. They just aren't happening yet. They are fundamentally beyond our control in that way. That's the *not-here future*. Getting a good grade is a *not-here future* event. That doesn't mean, though, that we must become passive and not plan or prepare for the test.

Our planning and anticipation for the test is our *storyline future*, which is fully a part of our experience now. The practical whole of nowflow is all that we can take care of and all that can make a practical difference, including our *storyline future* plans for the test and how that informs our preparations. Instead of feeling distracted or stressed about the future success or failure, we could prepare well using all the available information about what might happen, which is fully in nowflow, and this will even increase our chances of success. There is also no risk of downside with this understanding because we would simply be reminding ourselves of what is in our experience— and what isn't.

To make this guidance more clear, a teacher might advise students: "Taking the test itself and how well you do is the *not-here future*, so just take care of nowflow, including your *storyline future* plans and anticipation for the test—because that's all you can take care of." Or, more poetically, the teacher might say: "To *nowflow* action alone hast thou a right and never at all to its *not-here future* fruits."

Managing an empire

The Stoic philosopher and Roman emperor Marcus Aurelius wrote in his *Meditations*, "A man can lose neither the past nor the future; for how can one take from him that which is not his? ... Remember that man lives only in the present, in this fleeting instant; all the rest of his life is either past and gone, or not yet revealed."

To see an example of applying this advice in a challenging situation, let's consider how a coach might give this advice to help a team during the half-time of a sports game. The team was in the lead for the first part of the game, and then there was a series of mistakes and missed opportunities. As the team goes into the half-time break, the players may be struggling with regret over how they lost their advantage and fell behind the other team. They may also be worried about what will happen in the second half, such as anticipating with dread, "What if we lose the game after we had been so far ahead?"

The players at half-time need to reflect on what went wrong in the first half of the game. They need to get a strategy for how to do better in the second half. If the players feel caught up in their regrets about the past and worries for the future, this can be harder to do effectively. It's as if the past and the future are getting in the way of the players' ability to bring their best to this moment now as they meet, reflect, and plan.

The players might be somewhat puzzled, though, if coach Aurelius just told them to live "in the present, in this fleeting instant." After all, they don't just want temporary relief from regret and anxiety or a calmer state of mind. They want to win the game.

This highlights another potential confusion, which is that we might try to live in the now as if the past and the future aren't a part of our experience now. While reminding ourselves that "the past is gone," we may not realize that our *storyline past*—with all its richness of information about what has happened and what we've learned from it—is a part of our experience now. While reminding ourselves, that "the future is not yet revealed," we may not realize that our *storyline future*—with all its intentions, hopes, plans, worries, anticipations, or whatever form it may take—is influencing us right now, and we can influence our *storyline future* right now.

Coach Aurelius needs to help the players more clearly distinguish between what actually is in their experience and what isn't so that the players can be more effective in their handling of change going into the second half of the game. Let's see how coach Aurelius could apply an understanding of nowflow in order to give the team a locker-room talk along these lines. He might say, "The events of the first half of the game are gone, and the events of the second half game aren't in our experience yet. We cannot even get rid of the

gone past or the *not-here future* events. How could we
be rid of something that we don't have to begin with?
All that we can take care of is the practical whole of
nowflow—what is going on altogether right now."

This can help the players see how the past and the
future can't fundamentally get in the way of their fully
being now and taking care of what they can do in this
moment. It's not a matter of trying to block out—or
trying to be rid of—the events of those mistakes and
missed opportunities. The *gone past* events are gone.
The *not-here future* events are not here. With this clarity,
the players can more effectively use their *storyline past*
and *storyline future*, which are up to them now, to learn
from past events and plan for future ones.

Following "the way"
In the quotes from the *Bhagavad Gita* and Marcus
Aurelius' *Meditations,* we've seen how less confusion
about what is in our experience—and what isn't—is
practically helpful in our actions. When we applied
nowflow understanding to these quotations, we could
see how it is to nowflow action alone that we "have
a right," while the *gone past* or *not-here future* events
themselves are not even "ours to lose." By being more
clear on what is actually making a difference in our
actions, our actions can go better.

With nowflow understanding, we can see how it is
wise to take care of what we can take care of, which is

the practical whole of nowflow. Moment by moment, we can understand and feel—we can follow—the "way" of nowflow. The Buddhist sage Bodhidharma advised: "The wise don't regret the past or worry about the future. Nor do they cling to the present. But, moment by moment, they follow tao, the way."

With clarity about now as the practical whole, we can feel different emotionally. For example, past traumatic events themselves are not part of altogether nowflow. By perceiving this, we can feel more free from the burdens of regrets and pains about what happened. We could also perceive how change is an inherent part of now and so be more free from clinging to the current status of things. Instead of resisting change, we could manage change well by using the available information about change that is in nowflow. This could be a way towards peak performance. It could even be a way towards an unconditional sense of peace, whatever change might happen.

The Zen Master Dogen wrote, "Each moment is all being—each moment is the entire world. Reflect now whether any being or any world is left out of the present moment." This is an example of a more cryptic saying where there are different interpretations, some of which rely on going beyond a need for rational understanding. This may be one reason why such teachings tend to be regarded as spiritual but not always practical. Without a rational explanation, we

may feel uncertain whether such advice would work
in practical application.

This is another example of how we could apply an
understanding of nowflow. Dogen's quote could even
be surprisingly easy and straight-forward to para-
phrase in terms of nowflow understanding: Nowflow
is the whole of our experience—it is the whole of
everything that can make a practical difference. After
all, is there anything in our experience—anything that
can make a practical difference—that is not part of
nowflow?

Wisdom of less illusion

By looking at these sayings from various long-
standing traditions, we've seen how such wisdom has
been helpful for many people. We've also seen how
such sayings could have sometimes been misleading
because they are not more fully explained and there
are possible pitfalls, if taken too far, given different
interpretations.

If we choose, though, it is possible to see an under-
lying understanding of nowflow beneath the surface
of such practical, emotional, and even spiritual advice.
Change can be hard. Yet our experience of change
doesn't separate us from now. By understanding
nowflow as the practical whole, we can rationally
understand and explain to ourselves and others what
is in our experience (and what isn't) as we experience

change. Then all this wisdom on being now can always help us without any downside whatever the situation. It can help us see through the illusion that we are ever separating from now.

12

Present and Now

Present as part of now

People often use the words "present" and "now" interchangeably, as we saw in the traditional quotes from the previous chapter. We also saw how such sayings could be ambiguous and not always easy to know how to apply. In this chapter, we'll look at the relationship between "present" and "now" so we can clear up the potential for confusion between the two.

We have seen how being now isn't a matter of blocking out our storyline past and storyline future—because the storyline past and storyline future are now. But what about the present of our past-present-future storylines? We might still wonder whether being now is a matter of emphasizing the present of our storylines.

Now of the storyline's subject
Let's first take a look at the present of our storylines and how it relates to what is going on now. When

we want to catch a moving ball, for example, we are doing that through a storyline with the moving ball as the subject: The ball was over there (past), the ball is here (present), and the ball will be there (future). The present in this storyline is about the now of the storyline's subject: *the ball is here now.*

There can be other storylines in our experience—with other subjects—as we go to catch the moving ball. Instead of focusing just on the ball itself, for example, we could also notice our planning for where the ball will be. Perhaps we are currently planning that the ball will go long, but, a few moments ago, we were anticipating a shorter trajectory for the ball. We *were planning* (past) that the ball would be short, and currently we *are planning now* (present) that the ball will go farther. We may even anticipate how very soon we *will be planning* (future) with finer adjustments about where the ball will be. This shows that our planning, too, can be the subject of a past-present-future storyline. The present in this storyline is about the now of our planning: *our planning now is* (present) that the ball will go farther.

These are two examples of the present in storylines: *the ball is here now* and *our planning now is that the ball will go farther.* From these examples, we can see that the present depends on the subject of our storylines. In one storyline, the present is about the now of the ball. In another storyline, the present is about the now of our planning for where the ball will be.

Partial present—expanding

As we go to catch the moving ball, we may have many
storylines about many subjects, such as the ball, our
body, or our planning. We could also have a broader
subject of a storyline, such as our experience, action,
or situation. As we've seen, our sense of what is
"present" would depend on our storylines and their
subject. To some degree, we could use more or broader
subjects of storylines to feel that more of our experience is "the present." That could help "the present"
seem relatively more expansive and more whole, but
this partial sense would be limited.

"The present" of past-present-future is always part of
a past-present-future storyline about change and so
can't indicate the practical whole. Perceiving more and
more as the present would never fully reach nowflow
understanding, which is that the past and the future of
our storylines, as well as the present of our storylines,
are fully now. We might even feel this limitation. For
example, the present of a storyline by itself would not
inherently include change or our perception of the
flow of change.

Whole nowflow—enveloping

By contrast, nowflow inherently includes the flow of
change and encompasses the whole of all available
storylines, including the past and the future of
storylines as well as the present. We need and use the
past-present-future of our storylines as we manage
change. We experience the flow of change.

As we've seen, all of this can be enveloped in a sense of being now when we understand now as nowflow. The changing ball, our changing body, and our changing plans are all part of the practical whole of nowflow. In this all-encompassing way, we can use general nowflow understanding to help us more clearly feel in the now—and also in the flow—of altogether nowflow.

13

Meditation

Clearer perception of altogether nowflow

In this chapter, we'll look at applying nowflow understanding to mindfulness meditation practice from the Buddhist tradition. When discussing how nowflow understanding works for meditation, we briefly mentioned the samatha-vipassana practice of meditation where meditators can start by feeling a sense of "calm-abiding" with their breathing. As it says in the *Satipatthana Sutra* on mindfulness, "If I am breathing in, I feel that I am breathing in. If I am breathing out, I feel that I am breathing out." There is also encouragement simply to notice whether the breath is "long" or "short" without judging that one is better than the other: "If I am breathing long, I feel that I am breathing long. If I am breathing short, I feel that I am breathing short."

Instructions for mindfulness meditation often begin with this encouragement to pay attention to our experience of the breath as it is now. A meditator could use counting the breaths as an aid for continuing to give attention to her moment-by-moment experience of the breath. At the end of each exhale, she would count— one, two, three, etc.—up to ten and then begin again at one. When she notices that her mind has wandered off the breathing, she can practice letting the thoughts go with a non-judgmental attitude and bringing her mind back to the breath again.

Given these instructions for practice, it could seem as if the goal of meditation is excluding thoughts, especially thoughts about the past and the future. Meditators are often surprised by how much their minds are jumping around and how hard it can be for the "monkey mind" to follow these basic instructions of continuing to observe the breath. There could even be a quality of struggle or restriction as meditators try to focus just on the breath.

Some beginners can find meditation too difficult because of this. They may end up wresting with their mind and feeling as if they are doing it wrong because they have so many thoughts running through their head. Some meditators may get the benefit of feeling more calm, yet they may also be forcing their mind into a kind of narrow, concentrative state. They might feel as though they are looking through a narrow slit at the present of a specific storyline, such as *I am breathing now,* while blocking out the rest. Practically, it won't be possible to keep up this narrow concentration once off the meditation cushion and in everyday life.

Insight of now

There is additional guidance that meditators can follow if they read further in the *Satipatthana (Mindfulness) Sutra.* Verses of the sutra encourage mindfulness of various aspects of experience, starting with breath, body, and sensation, and leading to experience of mind. Below we'll apply nowflow understanding to these verses and see how they could guide a meditation practice towards insight, or vipassana, into the nature of our experience.

With now as nowflow, we can understand that there's change going on now, there's information about change going on now, and it's all going on altogether now—nowflow. To more clearly perceive this, we could start by noticing the now of one aspect of our experience that's going on. We could choose the now of our breathing going on as a convenient starting point.

By becoming more aware of the now of our breathing as movement and sensation in our body, our mind can gradually become more quiet so that we notice other parts of our experience that we may usually tend to take for granted. As we breathe, we can begin to feel our whole body going on now more fully. As it says in the *Sutra*, "I breathe in sensitive to my whole body. I breathe out sensitive to my whole body."

When feeling the now of our body, we are also feeling the action of our body—whatever it is doing now—more fully: "When walking, I feel that I am walking. When I am standing, I feel I am standing. When I am sitting, I feel that I am sitting. When lying down, I feel that I am lying down."

As we become more attuned to the now of our body, we can also notice more of the sensations and emotions going on now within the body. As it goes on to say in the *Sutra*, "If there is a pleasant feeling, I observe the pleasant feeling. If there is an unpleasant feeling, I observe the unpleasant feeling." Through these observations, we can come to more fully feel the now of sensations, signals, and emotions going on in our experience.

By observing the now of our breathing, body, senses, and emotions, we've also set the stage so that it's easier for us to observe the now of our mental activity that's going on in our mind. As it says in the *Sutra*, "When the mind is scattered, I perceive the mind is scattered. ... When the mind is centered, I perceive the mind is centered."

With nowflow understanding, we can know that even our most "scattered" thoughts are always "centered" in this broader sense: The mental activity that can make us feel caught up in the future or the past is happening in our mind now. As we come to more clearly see all that is going on in our experience now, we can also see that our storyline past and storyline future are fully part of what is happening now.

In this way, we can help ourselves see through the illusion of separation from nowflow. We could come to perceive our experience so clearly, yet we do not find anything in our experience that is separate from altogether nowflow. This can also be part of observing how nowflow of self arises, as more fully described in the forthcoming book, *Mindfulness-in-Action*.

Right there, right there

We often expect to be told how to fix ourselves and our problems by doing something different. Don't we need *try* to make something happen? These verses of the *Satipatthana (Mindfulness) Sutra* seem to be encouraging us to simply observe whatever is in our experience. They don't offer encouragement for us to breathe more deeply or to have more pleasant feelings. We're not instructed to try to get rid of scattered thoughts or to block out aspects of our experience because they don't make us feel peaceful and centered. The encouragement is simply to feel, observe, and be mindful of *whatever is going on* in our experience.

It could be puzzling how such a practice would be helpful. This might be a reason why it's tempting to try to fix ourselves by trying to "be now" in a restrictive way. For example, this is a common quote that some people think is misattributed to the Buddha: "Do not dwell in the past, do not dream of the future, but concentrate the mind on the present moment." This quote would make it seem as if partially blocking out thoughts about the past and the future is a solution that meditation is offering us. We have seen, though, that this would not be a practice that we could take with us off the meditation cushion and fully apply in every circumstance. It would not be an approach that could ultimately lead us to deeper insights about the nature of our experience.

By contrast, this is a saying of the Buddha from the *Bhaddekaratta Sutra*: "What is past is left behind. The future is as yet unreached. Whatever quality is present, you clearly see, right there, right there." As we've come to understand, the *gone past* events and the *not-here future* events are not now—completely. All of our experience is completely included—right there, right there—in altogether nowflow, including our past-present-future storylines about change. That insight would always apply. It would always help us whatever we're doing.

14

Daily Life

Taking care of everything altogether nowflow

Through the ages, as we've seen, there's been wise encouragement on the value of being now. We might wonder, though, about advice that comes from monks or yogis who may not have the typical demands of jobs, families, and other daily-life responsibilities. Without a rational explanation of now as the practical whole, we might question whether such insights would be helpful for a monk or a yogi but not for someone who is "living in the world."

In terms of running late to an important meeting, for instance, someone might agree that it's good to live in the "here and now." Yet, she may feel unsure about what that really means for her when applied to getting to a meeting. She might try to balance the practical need of managing actions for future events with (what she may consider to be) a deeper, inner need of "being now." Helpful as this may be to some degree, this can also reinforce the sense that we have to choose between a fundamental priority in life, such as choosing between outer results or inner peace: Do we prioritize taking care of the "doing" for future events *or* taking care of the "being" of now?

By understanding nowflow as the practical whole, we can see that there isn't a fundamental tradeoff we have to make. It doesn't come down to a choice between feeling more fully now vs. handling more of what is practical in our action. After all, everything that is practical in action is included in nowflow. By more fully perceiving all that is in our experience now, we could actually take better care of all that can make a practical difference.

Reminding of always practical whole

As we go about our daily lives, we're needing to manage and track various changes. What happened earlier? What's going to happen later? When there's stressful emphasis on the storyline past or storyline future, we sometimes can feel and act as if we are somehow separating from what is now. All these personal "histories" and "forecasts" can feel like they are interfering in our fuller experience of what is going on now.

As we've discussed, a meditation practice with nowflow understanding can give us a way to see through the illusion of separation from now. If thoughts come up about what we did yesterday, we can notice that we are now remembering our personal "history" of that day. If thoughts come up about what we will do, we can notice that we are now planning our personal "forecast" for the day ahead. Even if we feel more stressed and separate from now because of regrets for the past or worries about the future, we also can notice that we are regretting now and we are worrying now. By coming to know our experience better, we "uncover" how it is going on altogether nowflow.

Let's see how we might remind ourselves of this as we try to get to our meeting on time. To start, we may need an easy reminder to feel more connected to what's going on now. Perhaps we take a couple of mindful breaths: *I am breathing in now, I am breathing out now.* This can help us begin to feel the now of our body more fully while we are standing on the street corner: *I am standing here now.*

As we feel the now of our body, we could also begin to observe our worry and anxiety as sensations happening now. We might even start to notice the stressed-out thoughts running through our mind— now—about what will happen. When thoughts come up again about how we will be late, we can observe this storyline future—*I will be late*—as going on now in our mind.

Now includes our storyline future for getting to the meeting as well as everything else that's going on in our experience now, including the perception that lets us most quickly and safely cross the street. Instead of acting as if there is some fundamental choice we have to make between experiencing *I am here now* and *I will be late*, we can more freely and effectively prioritize all our available past-present-future storyline information. As important as it may be to get to the meeting on time, it is not as important as surviving the crossing of the street when there is an oncoming car. Instead of being "blinded by stress" about the future, we can more fully respond and act moment by moment in ways that allow our action to be more optimal.

By being mindful of our own experience as it is, we can help ourselves perceive how it is happening altogether nowflow. We can be on the sidewalk, heading towards our meeting, with a sense of the now of the traffic around us, the now of our body, the now of our emotions, and even the now of our mental activity, including the now of planning—our storyline future— for getting to the meeting. All of this is affecting our action right now.

Applying fully in life

As we've seen, there is not a fundamental tradeoff we must make between the "doing" of managing change with our sense of past-present-future vs. the "being" of just being now. All that's going on now—altogether nowflow—encompasses whatever can make a practical difference, including our sense of past-present-future for managing changes in our lives.

This clarity of perception helps us to take care of what we can. We can be more responsive to whatever can make a difference—the practical whole of our action. We could maneuver around traffic safely and speedily. We could come up with alternate routes and select the best one given the current conditions. Seeing through the illusion of separation from nowflow is something that we can fully apply in life without practical tradeoffs or downsides.

In this way, all of life can be an opportunity to practice clearer perception of the practical whole of nowflow. Whatever the situation, we can take care of everything by taking care of nowflow. By understanding and more clearly perceiving this, we can manage change more optimally. Feeling in the now of altogether nowflow allows us to perform at our potential, whether that is getting to a meeting on time or any kind of challenge we may face.

15

Peak Performance

In the flow of altogether nowflow

It can seem quite mysterious. During moments of peak performance, people sometimes report feeling a deep sense of "flow" and connection to what's going on now, even as they may be doing something difficult. Reports of this kind of experience date back thousands of years. For example, in the stories of the Taoist philosopher Zhuangzi, there are accounts of butchers and woodcarvers who could achieve extraordinary results even as their actions felt effortless.

Athletes, artists, and other performers today continue to report how their performance can improve—sometimes dramatically—when they feel "in the flow." This kind of improvement can raise questions. It may seem puzzling how a performance can suddenly feel more effortless even as it goes better.

Traditionally, people would sometimes attribute their peak-performance experiences to something mysterious or even supernatural at work, such as their action arising from spirit or an unexplained force such as qi. Even today with the knowledge we have, these experiences of being "in the flow" can seem hard to understand.

We've seen, though, how we can more clearly perceive *altogether nowflow* and how this can help us manage change more optimally. We've seen how feeling more fully in the nowflow can help us take care of everything practical in our action so that we can achieve the best outcomes. Given this understanding of nowflow as the practical whole, let's see how we could explain the flow state of peak performance.

Informing us now

First, let's see how a surfer might run into some trouble with her performance if she feels caught up in a storyline future about how her surfing will go. For example, she may have some fixed expectation or intention about the upcoming move she should make and how she should do it. Because the surfer is feeling more caught up in the future of her past-present-future storyline about change, she might feel as if she's partially disconnected from her experience as it is happening now.

With nowflow understanding, though, we've seen that past-present-future storylines and change are all part of nowflow. The surfer's experience of *I am making this move* and *I will soon make that move* are both happening now. Both are going on in her mind now as part of her past-present-future storyline about her moving body: I *was* making that move, I *am* making this move, and I *will* soon make that move.

The surfer can only ride the wave now. If the surfer could feel how all of her experience—including information about what *has happened* and what *will happen*—is happening as part of altogether nowflow, she could feel in the flow of change without a sense of separation from now.

When there is less illusion of separation from nowflow, there is less illusion getting in the way of the surfer feeling how everything in her experience—including her planning and intentions—are flowing altogether now. She could feel how all this available information is informing her current action now. With this fuller sense of perceiving and responding to all that contributes to her action, her performance would naturally improve as a result. In this way, clearer perception of altogether nowflow can explain the improved performance of the flow state.

Seeing "impossible" possible
This also applies to cases where very challenging feats can become doable. For example, a martial artist typically won't be able to generate much power at short range, such as when the fist is an inch away

from the target. Even when martial art masters could demonstrate this seemingly impossible feat in tests of power, it was difficult to explain how they were able to have such results without crediting mysterious or supernatural forces.

By applying nowflow understanding to these cases, we can see how it is possible for a martial artist to use all that's available—in the flow of each moment—to better inform and manage their action of punching. For example, if a martial artist is more caught up in her storyline future about making a powerful punch, she won't be able to fully feel what is contributing to her action now, including the flow of earth's gravity and support, the flow of her whole body and all its signals and sensations, and even the flow of her own awareness and intention. By contrast, if even her intention to punch feels included in the flow of altogether nowflow, her punch can be more powerful at close range. As she feels less and less illusion of separation from altogether nowflow, the action can become so effortless that she may feel almost as if the punching is "happening for her."

This fuller sense of being in the flow of action is something that students can practice in meditative movement, such as the form practices of the martial art of tai chi. Students can then apply this clarity of perception to martial art moves and see the practical results. They can test for themselves how clearer perception of nowflow helps them perform more optimally, such as being able to generate powerful punches at a short range of an inch.

This is just one example of applying nowflow understanding to one's discipline, such as the martial arts. As we've seen, nowflow understanding is general and so applies to any situation. Whatever one's discipline, job, or role, one can apply nowflow understanding to have less illusion of separation in one's action. This can lead to improved performance and even approach the flow state where one clearly perceives how everything in action is flowing together—now. Further examples of such practice and guidance are introduced in the *Nowflow Mindfulness Primer* linked at the back of this book, while a full account will be in the forthcoming book, *Mindfulness-in-Action*.

Flow of change now

As we've seen, if someone is effectively taking care of all that is contributing to their action, they would be perceiving and responding with a sense of being in the flow of altogether nowflow. When there is less illusion of separation from nowflow, people would naturally perceive the flow of nowflow more clearly. After all, now*flow*—but not nowshape—is the practical whole of all that can make a difference in our actions.

It's not surprising, then, that people came to use the word "flow" to describe a state of peak performance.

Reports of the flow state sometimes also describe the experience as feeling all-encompassing, whole, or even "timeless." Even though these reports may sound strange or puzzling, we can see such descriptions in light of nowflow understanding. It is possible that accounts of all-encompassing wholeness while in the flow state are descriptions of what it feels like to more clearly perceive altogether nowflow. Even reports about an altered sense of time or "no time" can be consistent with nowflow understanding and with physics, as is discussed further in the appendix Nowflow and Time.

People might talk about how they were—or weren't—"in the flow" during their performance. Because they think in terms of being "in it" or not, they might try to be "in the flow" during their performances. Paradoxically, when people try to be "in the flow," they often find that the flow state eludes them more. This can make the flow state seem even more tenuous, rare, and difficult to achieve.

We have seen, though, that nowflow has a deeper meaning than these kinds of conditional experiences. Nowflow is beyond *more* or *less* because it is simply the way our experience is always happening. It is not something we try to get more of or achieve more of, which can mislead people who want to experience more "flow" for peak performance. Now*flow* is an underlying, unconditional nature of reality. With less illusion of separation from nowflow, the flow of nowflow is simply revealed. This may be why the flow state can feel like the opposite of trying or achieving.

With an understanding of nowflow, even if a sense of being "in the flow" happens to us almost accidentally, we could gain more insight from that experience. We could view the flow state of peak performance as a chance to feel with more clarity how our experience is actually flowing altogether now. We could know that we are glimpsing what it's like to have less illusion that we are separating from nowflow as we experience change.

We also would not have to rely only on such glimpses during peak performance or feel that they are somehow beyond what we could practice and experience in everyday life. As we'll see more generally in the next chapter, there are ways to practice the clearer perception of nowflow. We can help ourselves feel in the flow of all our action because we can understand that we are always in the flow of altogether nowflow.

16

Applying to All Actions

A look ahead to general
mindfulness and relaxation

Because change never actually separates us from
being in the nowflow, we can apply this clarity of
perception to all our action. Feeling in the now and
in the flow of altogether nowflow would allow us
to better manage and respond to all the changes of
our lives—whatever we do. What would it be like
to apply this simple and general understanding of
nowflow to our lives? Even as we might do the same
outward actions of, say, getting to a meeting, surfing,
or sitting in meditation, there could be a fundamentally different way that we would approach getting
better at those actions.

Instead of striving to "do more," "be more," or "make
something happen," we could find improvement by
allowing ourselves to feel the way we already are and
the way things already are happening. We can feel
better and do better by feeling and doing less and
less as if we are partially separating from nowflow.

Because we are already always in the now and in the flow of altogether nowflow, that's the nature of progress, as we apply nowflow understanding.

This approach to improvement in meditation, peak performance, and daily life can also provide a fundamental safety. While particular techniques, methods, or principles might have advantages and disadvantages in different cases, a general understanding of nowflow can always be a guide towards improvements without downsides. As we've seen, there are no rational conflicts or practical tradeoffs. Less illusion of separation from nowflow is always helpful because we are, after all, always fully in nowflow.

Overview: Mindfulness and Relaxation-in-action

As a further guide in applying nowflow understanding, we can also apply a general understanding of relaxation-in-action and mindfulness-in-action. As we'll see, we can completely be mindful and completely be relaxed, and this will only help us practically if we understand mindfulness and relaxation generally.

First, let's see why someone might think that we need to hold back on mindfulness and not apply it fully to every action. Because mindfulness practice can emphasize observing our experience just as it is, we may wonder how to fully apply this when we are in a situation that requires us to make decisions and form

intentions for action. For example, if we want to bring
about a change, we might feel puzzled if someone asks
us to simply observe ourselves or a situation without
any judgment of it as good or bad.

Also, we may feel some doubt if someone encourages
us to fully relax when we are trying to accomplish
something difficult. We may typically associate relaxation as a kind of "not-doing"—or even as "doing
nothing at all." For example, we might wish to be
more relaxed yet feel that we cannot because we've
got too much to do. We may tend to think that we can
finally, more completely relax only once the important
action is over.

These are examples of how we may try to balance
relaxation and mindfulness with other concerns
because we assume that there's some balance that we
have to get right. We might think that we shouldn't
be "too relaxed" or "overly mindful" when we need
to bring about a crucial change or when undertaking
a goal-oriented action that is important to us. This
is similar to how (before understanding nowflow as
the practical whole) we may have thought that we
couldn't fully "be now" when we needed to get something important done.

In this book, *Way of Now*, we've seen how we can
always fully apply an understanding of now as
nowflow without conundrums. Below is a preview of

an understanding of mindfulness and relaxation that
we can also fully and generally apply in all action. In
the books *Mindfulness-in-Action* and *Relaxation-in-Action*, there will be further explanation of these topics,
while the essential understanding is summarized here.

Preview: Relaxation-in-action

An athlete or other performer might find that their
performance goes better if they feel more relaxed
prior to or even during the performance. They might
aim to be suitably relaxed for the performance or to
balance relaxation with other considerations. With this
approach to relaxation, it is as if there is a limit to how
much relaxation can help them practically and they
don't want to take it too far.

With relaxation-in-action, complete relaxation is
always suitable for any action or situation. In other
words, the more fully relaxed we are, the better our
action goes. This can sound somewhat counterin-
tuitive at first, but it is possible to understand in a
straightforward way. Relaxation can be generally
understood as a necessary condition for optimal
action.

For a given action, there are two ways we can do it
better. We can do more of what is helpful, and we can
do less of what is not helpful. We could say that these
are the two practical components of optimal action:
- Doing what is correct
- *Not-doing* what is incorrect

Relaxation-in-action is *not-doing what is interfering in our own action*. It is one of the two practical components of optimal action. With this understanding of relaxation, our action always goes better when we are more fully relaxed.

By contrast, if we are thinking of relaxation as just "not-doing" (or as "not-doing anything at all"), then we can only relax so far practically. For example, with this typical sense of relaxation, we might think that completely relaxing our physical body would mean not engaging any of our skeletal muscles, yet we would need to engage our muscles in order to lift something. But what if we think of relaxation as *not-doing what is interfering in our own action*?

We only need to engage those muscles that are helpful for our given action and don't need to engage any muscles that are not helpful. While doing a biceps curl, *not engaging* the antagonistic muscle of the triceps (since that would interfere in the strength of bending our arm) would allow us to lift something heavier. With relaxation-in-action, we will actually be physically stronger the more relaxed we are by *not-doing what is interfering in our own action*. The greater our relaxation, the better our action goes.

Relaxation-in-action can help us to see what is often overlooked as we seek to improve our actions. When we want to do better, we can tend to focus on how to do more and more. Relaxation-in-action is about doing less and less in order to do better. By seeing both components of optimal action, we can see how it is not a matter of just one or the other. Practically, it is by taking into account *both* components of optimal action—the *doing* and the *not-doing*—that we can approach what is possible for us in our actions.

The peak performances of athletes and artists can give us a glimpse of how this is the case. The greatest runners or boxers, for instance, don't tend to show the signs of strain and tightness that we would expect from such strenuous physical activities. Such performances can seem effortless, even as the performers are doing feats that are near the limit of human potential.

With an understanding of relaxation-in-action, we can see that an athlete can be the best only if she is excellent at both components for optimal action: excellent at doing what is helpful and also excellent at relaxing—*not-doing* what is unhelpful for her actions. Because the athlete is more fully relaxed, the performance both looks more effortless and also goes better. The relaxation-in-action demonstrated in the athlete's effortless performance is actually a necessary condition for performing at her full potential.

This is one way we can understand wu-wei (literally *not-doing*) in Eastern philosophy, which is sometimes translated as "doing by not-doing." Though this can

seem enigmatic or puzzling, an explanation of wu-wei
can be similar to an understanding of relaxation-in-action: by *not-doing* what is interfering in our own action,
the doing of our action goes better.

There is a verse in the *Tao Te Ching* by the Taoist
philosopher Laozi that states, "wu wei er wu bu wei 無
為而無不為," which could be translated as *"not-doing*
so that nothing is left undone." This can be another
way of expressing that wu-wei, or relaxation-in-action,
is a necessary condition for optimal action. If the
performer is still interfering in her own action (by
doing too much of what is not helpful), then she will
fall short of what is possible for her. Things that could
have been done will be "left undone."

With this general understanding of relaxation, we can
discover the benefits of doing less and less of what is
not helpful in everything we are and do. We know that
we can completely relax, whatever we may be doing,
and that *not-doing of the interference in our own action*
will always help our action be more optimal.

With this understanding of relaxation, we can also
see why relaxation is important in applying nowflow
understanding. Because nowflow is always uncondi-
tionally the practical whole, we actually can't do more
to be more in the nowflow. This is how generalized
relaxation—the *not-doing* of interference—becomes
more important when applying unconditional under-

standing of the way things always are. It is by having *less interference* in our own perception of nowflow—by *not-doing* as if we are separating from nowflow—that we can feel better and do better.

Preview: Mindfulness-in-action

With mindfulness-in-action, we can understand mindfulness as relaxing the interference in our clearer perception or awareness. After all, why it is helpful to emphasize simply observing one's own experience *as it is*, without the judgments we may tend to have about it? One underlying reason is that our pre-judgments can interfere in our fuller awareness.

Awareness lets us know what is going on. It's input—input to our mind. With that information about what's going on, we can make decisions and plans about what we intend to do. Our intention is output—the output of instructions for our actions. This is a basic pattern of how we manage change: based on the input of awareness, the output of intention arises. There is this natural order of input-output or awareness-intention.

Though awareness "comes first" in this natural order, our intention can tend to interfere in our awareness, especially when we are more stressed because of fixed pre-judgements about what we want. Our interfering intentions can tend to be about how things should be, rather than being more fully informed by how things

are. When we don't want something to be happening
(because it's "bad") or when we really want something
to happen (because it's "good"), we tend to interfere in
our fuller awareness of all that is going on.

Sometimes we may act almost as if intention comes
first before awareness. When we're acting as if
our *out*put of intention comes before the *in*put of
awareness, our awareness cannot as fully inform our
intention. This is how our more judgmental or overly
strong intentions can interfere in our awareness.

Given this tendency, we can see mindfulness as
helping us to "restore" the natural order of awareness
first, then intention. While we need discerning judgment and informed intentions to guide our actions,
we don't need the output of intention to interfere
in the fuller input of awareness. This is one reason
why sometimes observing our experience just as it
is, without trying to judge it or fix it as much, can be
transformative. By not interfering in our awareness
quite as much, we can solve difficulties in how we
perceive, feel, and act because we are giving awareness a chance to more fully play its role as input.

With an understanding of mindfulness-in-action, we
can be as mindful without pre-judgement as we can
be, and this *not interfering in our own awareness* will
always help our action go better. Mindfulness-in-action allows us to have fuller awareness that can

give rise to better informed intentions and resulting actions.

People may variously describe this as having less judgment or even as having "no intention." Those can be helpful descriptions of what it can feel like to more fully allow intention to arise from awareness. When our intentions feel in the flow of responding to our awareness, our actions can be more effortless even as they go better, such as in the flow state of peak performance. With this general understanding, there can be various ways of practicing for the flow state, as more fully described in the book *Mindfulness-in-Action*. (A primer on nowflow mindfulness is linked in the resource section.)

We can also see why generalized mindfulness is important in applying nowflow understanding. Sometimes people associate mindfulness with concentration or focus on some *part* of their experience. Mindfulness practices often start with instructions for consciously noticing some particular aspect, such as the breath or other sensations, sights, or sounds, which are the input of our senses. Generalized mindfulness, or mindfulness-in-action, helps us to feel more of the *whole*—as well as the parts—of our experience because it applies generally. Less interference in our fuller awareness can apply to our subconscious as well as conscious mind. In practice, this is how we can have fuller perception of altogether nowflow.

A curious kind of journey

As we've seen, we can help ourselves have less of the illusion of separating from now by allowing ourselves to *mindfully* perceive our experience as it is—which is altogether nowflow. With clearer perception, we can further *relax* the interference that makes us feel and act as if we are separating from now. Through mindfulness-in-action and relaxation-in-action, we can find improvement by doing less in our perception and in our action that makes it seem as if we are not already fully in the nowflow.

This may be different from what we are used to as we seek improvement in our lives. We are used to going on a journey where we are heading for a different destination. We are used to transformations where we hope to become something different than what we are already. The application of nowflow understanding isn't like this.

We are already always in the nowflow. It is a journey to where we are. It is a transformation to what we are.

17

Nowflow as Practical Whole

Simple, rational, and practical
guide to all action

———————

A child watches the changing clouds. We toss a ball
in a game of catch. Change—it's so basic to our experience. Yet we can tend to experience it through some
illusion: We may feel and act as if our experience of
change can partially separate us from now.

To experience and manage change, we have past-present-future storylines. We could be lying in the peace
and quiet of our bedroom at night. We could also be
experiencing a storyline future about all that we need
to get done tomorrow. Because of "the future," we
may feel as if we partially separate from the "here and
now." Perhaps we even release stress hormones as if
we are already dealing with tomorrow's events now
when right now we just need a good night's sleep. As
we've seen, this is an example of the illusion that we
are separating from now as we manage change with
past-present-future storylines about change.

In this book, we have seen a rational understanding
of nowflow as the practical whole. Now as nowflow is
enough to include the flow of change, our storylines,
our experience of change—all that can make a practical difference. By coming to know our experience
of change more clearly, we can see that change never
separates us from now. We are always in altogether
nowflow, and we can more fully perceive this is so.
*There is change going on. There is information about
change going on with past-present-future storylines. It's
all happening together now as part of the practical whole of
nowflow.* Instead of feeling and doing as if we are not
fully now, we can allow ourselves to more clearly feel
in the now and in the flow of altogether nowflow.

There's no exception to when this clarity might help
us because we are not having to balance conflicting
practical considerations in order to be in nowflow.
Applying nowflow understanding is not a matter of
gaining more peace of mind at the expense of attaining
practical outcomes that we want. It's not a matter
of blocking out aspects of our experience—such as
the past and the future—in order to try to be now.
Nowflow understanding can guide us to see that
we are already always now, however we might be
perceiving and managing what happens in our experience.

In this way, an understanding of nowflow serves as
a simple, rational, and practical guide for all of expe-

rience and action. We don't need one sense of being now for our meditation practice and another for taking care of the responsibilities of our lives. We don't need an "extraordinary" kind of being now for when we are in the flow state during some special activity and an "ordinary" kind of being now as we do our everyday routines. We can fully apply nowflow understanding in all life experience.

Past-present-future now

In coming to this conundrum-free understanding of what is now, we first saw that there are two pasts and two futures. In this way, we could be clear that the storyline future is *about* "the future that isn't here yet," but our storyline future itself is already completely here and now. The storyline future that is informing us now and making a practical difference now cannot separate us from now.

We've also seen how the storyline past is *about* "the past that is gone," but the storyline past itself isn't gone. The storyline past is completely here and now so that, even while the storyline past usefully informs us, we can feel free from the burdens of past events themselves. We can have this clarity about what is—and what is not—in our experience now.

Altogether now*flow*

Historically, there have been people who considered whether now could "be everything." Without a rational explanation, though, there could be different interpretations with possible contradictions and conundrums. For example, it wouldn't work practically to think that tomorrow's event itself is part of "everything" that is now. As we've seen as well, it wouldn't work rationally to think that everything that matters could be included in now as nowshape.

By understanding now as nowflow, we can rationally understand now as the practical whole of everything that can make a difference. We can understand— consistently and simply—the inseparability of now and change. We've seen how this understanding is also consistent with physics and biology, as well as being fully applicable in all of life experience.

Way of nowflow

Now as nowflow includes the flow of change. It includes all available past-present-future storyline information about change. Nowflow is the practical whole. By understanding this, we can see why being "in the now" and "in the flow" for millennia have been part of the answer to the question: how can we live better?

How can we be more free from suffering? How can we realize our full human potential? Even though being "in the now" and "in the flow" have long been part of humanity's seeking, some practical and rational conundrums seemed to remain. By understanding now as nowflow, we have a rational foundation so that we can more effectively and safely guide ourselves on our own varied journeys.

When we more clearly perceive nowflow as the practical whole by feeling in the now and in the flow of nowflow, everything can work better for us even as we suffer less from the illusion of separation—no matter what the situation. Because nowflow is the whole of all that can make a practical difference, we don't need to—and can't—separate from now. However much we may sometimes be struggling through a sense of separation, whatever we are experiencing is fully right here, right now.

We do not have to strive to more fully be in altogether nowflow. All of our experience—including the flow of change and including our past-present-future storylines—are already fully in nowflow. This is an understanding that can guide our better perception for better action in all of life. Daily life can be a meditation as we live in the now, and daily life can also be a peak performance as we feel in the flow. This can be a way towards a better life for us all.

This is an option available to us. It is a way—the way of nowflow.

Appendix

Nowflow and Time

While in the flow state of peak performance, some people have reported that they experience an altered sense of time. This can seem strange or mysterious, yet we can look at the question of time more generally in light of an understanding that change is included in now—nowflow. In this appendix, we will look at how an alternative interpretation of time is possible with a "change-first" or nowflow view. This can also shed light on why some Eastern and Western philosophers, and even some scientists, have questioned whether or not time is an illusion.

This kind of questioning of time can be surprising, especially in our modern-day life, because our use of time so often pervades our days. In order to measure how long things take and coordinate with others, we need the practical use of time. In its practical usage, *time* helps us to quantify and compare changes more easily. This can be seen as similar to how *length* helps us to quantify and compare spaces more easily.

Use of length and time

Let's see this in an everyday example, such as wanting to put a sofa in our living room. If we are not sure whether the sofa will fit, we could help ourselves in this comparison of spaces by using a ruler to measure the length of the living room and the length of the sofa. In this example, there are the *spaces* of the sofa and the room. There is a *ruler*, a standard, chosen thing with spatial extent that we use to measure other things that take up space. By using the ruler to measure the space of the room and the sofa, we get the numbers—the *lengths*—that are helpful in our practical comparisons. From this example, we can see how *space* is "first." Then the use of a *ruler* gives the numerical *length* values that are practical for us as we decide whether the sofa will fit in the room.

> space (first)
> ruler
> length

With this space(first)-ruler-length pattern in mind, let's turn to an example where we're dealing with change. In this scenario, we are backpacking and want to get to the next resupply camp before our food runs out. We could help ourselves in this comparison between the change of food supply and the change of location by putting some numbers to them. We could use the sun, for example, as a clock that measures both the change in food supply and change in location. Then we'd know that we have enough food for 6 days—6 "suns"—while it takes us 5 "suns" to get there. This comparison helps us to know that we won't go hungry.

In this example, there are the *changes* of the food supply and our location. There is a *clock*, which is a chosen changing thing such as the sun, that we use to measure other changing things. By using the clock to measure the changes, we get the numbers—the *times*—that are helpful in our practical comparisons.

> change (first)
> clock
> time

From this example, we can see how *change* is "first." Then the use of a *clock* gives us the numerical *time* values that are practical for us as we decide whether we will finish our food before or after we get to the resupply camp. As we can see from this example, change(first)-clock-time is a description of our practical use of time. This is how we get the numbers that can be useful in quantifying and comparing changes. It is analogous to the space(first)-ruler-length pattern, as shown below.

> space (first)   change (first)
> ruler   clock
> length   time

As we've just seen, *time* in our practical usage can be numerical values, measured via *clocks*, that allow us to compare *changes*. This is analogous to our practical usage of *length* as numerical values, measured by *rulers*, that allow us to compare *spaces*. This interpretation can apply in any situation, including scientific measurements, and gives the same numerical time values.

In scientific measurements, more accurate rulers and clocks are used. For example, instead of the clock of the rising and setting sun, scientific measurements of change might use a vibrating cesium atom as a clock. Whatever is used, numerical time values are measurements made with a clock that is a *changing thing*. This is analogous to how numerical length values come from our use of some chosen *thing with spatial extent*, such as a meter stick.

With this description of our practical use of time in mind, we can see how—just as with length values—there is nothing particularly mysterious about time values in terms of our practical usage of time. We experience space and change. We measure space and change with rulers and clocks and use numerical length and time values. With this in mind, we would view space and change as being fundamental. In the change(first)-clock-time view, we're thinking that time values from clocks are measurements of *change*.

A priori time

More typically, though, we may first assume that there is time—what we can call *a priori* time—that "comes first." In the time(first) view, we're thinking that time values are measurements of *a priori* time and that space and *a priori* time are fundamental, as shown below.

space (first)	a priori time (first)
ruler	clock
length	time

The assumption of *a priori* time doesn't affect the practical role of clocks and numerical time values. As we can see in the side-by-side comparison below, the numerical time values and practical use of time are the same in both the time(first) and the change(first) view. Because both are equivalent in terms of giving the same numbers in everyday life and scientific measurements, both are valid views.

A priori time(first) view	Change(first) view
space	a priori time (first)	space	change (first)
ruler	*clock*	*ruler*	*clock*
length	*time*	*length*	*time*

Time(first) and illusion of separating from nowflow

Though both views are equivalent in terms of the practical use of clocks and numerical time values, there may be advantages or disadvantages to the

change(first) view and the *a priori* time(first) view in
different situations. Let's see what it is like to use the
typical time(first) view in the example where we are
running late to a meeting.

When we look at our watch, we would assume that
our watch is giving us information about how much
time (which we are thinking of as *a priori* time) we
have left: Do we have enough (*a priori*) time in which
to get to the meeting place before that event "arrives"
at 10 o'clock? We may tend to interpret our experience
as if we are dealing with an upcoming meeting "out
ahead of us" in (*a priori*) future time, which is not
now. This can make us more prone to illusion that
we are partially separating from now. For most of
us in modern-day life, this may be the usual way we
process our use of time.

Change(first) and the practical whole of nowflow

As we've seen earlier in this book, all our managing
of change for an upcoming event is part of nowflow,
while the upcoming event itself is not part of nowflow.
Our managing of change can include our use of clocks
and time values, which are also part of nowflow. We
can feel this more clearly with a change(first) view
of time because the meaning of time is included in
nowflow, which includes change.

This can explain how the change(first) view of time
does not tend to cause illusion of separation from

now. For example, if we are running late to a meeting and look at our watch, we could see our watch as a changing thing—now—that gives us helpful numerical values for past-present-future storylines about change, which are also all part of nowflow.

As described in the chapter on peak performance, we can manage change more effectively if we have less illusion of separation from the practical whole of nowflow. It's not surprising, then, that people report feeling an altered sense of time—or even a sense of "no time"—while in the flow state of peak performance. They may feel less or even no illusion of separation while they experience and manage change, and this feels different because their typical sense of the past and the future in *a priori* time usually comes with some illusion of separation from now.

With this understanding, an experience of an altered sense of time would not have to be strange or inexplicable. We've seen how a change(first) view of time is also natural and rational, as well as being in agreement with the typical *a priori* time in practical usage. We may feel an experiential difference because the time(first) view is more prone to the illusion of separation from the practical whole of nowflow, while the change(first) view is more conducive to feeling in the flow and in the now of altogether nowflow.

This understanding of an alternate sense of time also opens up possibilities for further practice and application. Because nowflow is the practical whole, our performance improves when we more clearly perceive altogether nowflow, and a more conducive view of time for that would help us. As will be described in the forthcoming book *Mindfulness-in-Action*, we can incorporate a change(first) view of time to help us have less illusion of separation from nowflow and so more easily feel in the flow of peak performance.

List of quotation references

Ch. 6 Nowflow
"Ever changing water flows over those stepping into
the same river."
Heraclitus, fragment B12
Translation by Mackenzie Hawkins for *Way of Now*

Ch. 11 Wisdom through the Ages
"To action alone hast thou a right and never at all to its
fruits."
Bhagavad Gita, chapter 2, verse 47
Translation by Sarvepalli Radhakrishnan

"For a man can lose neither the past nor the future; for
how can one take from him that which is not his?"
Meditations by Marcus Aurelius, Book II, 14
Translation by M. H. Morgan

"Remember that man lives only in the present, in this
fleeting instant; all the rest of his life is either past and
gone, or not yet revealed."
Meditations by Marcus Aurelius, Book III, 10
Translation by Maxwell Staniforth

"The wise don't regret the past or worry about the future. Nor do they cling to the present. But, moment by moment, they follow tao, or 'the way.'"
Bodhidharma's *Wake-up Sermon*
Adapted from a translation by Bill Porter "Red Pine"

"Each moment is all being—each moment is the entire world. Reflect now whether any being or any world is left out of the present moment."
Shobogenzo "Uji" by Dogen
Adapted from a translation by Norman Waddell and Abe Masao

Ch. 13 Meditation
Paraphrasing quotations from *Satipatthana Sutta*.
Based on translations by Thanissaro Bhikkhu and Thich Nhat Hanh

"What is past is left behind. The future is as yet unreached. Whatever quality is present, you clearly see, right there, right there."
Bhaddekaratta Sutta
Translation by Thanissaro Bhikkhu

Ch. 16 Applying to All Actions
"Not-doing [what is interfering in our own action] so that nothing is left undone [meaning that not-doing, or relaxation, is a necessary condition for optimal action]."
Tao Te Ching, Verse 48, by Laozi
Translation by Wonchull Park for *Way of Now*

Links: Nowflow Mindfulness Primer
& additional resources

Nowflow Mindfulness Primer

5 levels for practice (with cartoons)
https://www.nowflow.org/nm5

Updates about forthcoming books

https://www.nowflow.org/updates

Visit website for additional resources

https://www.nowflow.org

About the Authors

Wonchull Park is a tai chi master and physicist. With a rational understanding of now (nowflow), generalized mindfulness (nowflow mindfulness) and generalized relaxation (wuwei), he teaches a comprehensive understanding of optimal action in all aspects of human endeavor, including meditation, martial arts, and daily life. Master Park founded Wuwei Tai Chi School (www.wuweitaichi.org) while a principal research physicist at Princeton University.

Mackenzie Hawkins teaches meditation, tai chi, and optimal action with her Learning the Mind (www.learningthemind.org) program. She studied the history of science and philosophy at Princeton University.

Reach the authors with comments
and questions via email:
      nowflow.mackenzie@gmail.com
      nowflow.park@gmail.com

Made in the USA
Columbia, SC
24 September 2020